FIVE
RULES FOR
REBELLION

FIVE RULES FOR REBELLION

LET'S CHANGE THE WORLD OURSELVES

SOPHIE WALKER

Published in the UK in 2020
by Icon Books Ltd, Omnibus Business Centre,
39–41 North Road, London N7 9DP
email: info@iconbooks.com
www.iconbooks.com

Sold in the UK, Europe and Asia
by Faber & Faber Ltd, Bloomsbury House,
74–77 Great Russell Street,
London WC1B 3DA or their agents

Distributed in the UK, Europe and Asia
by Grantham Book Services,
Trent Road, Grantham NG31 7XQ

Distributed in Australia and New Zealand
by Allen & Unwin Pty Ltd,
PO Box 8500, 83 Alexander Street,
Crows Nest, NSW 2065

Distributed in South Africa
by Jonathan Ball, Office B4, The District,
41 Sir Lowry Road, Woodstock 7925

Distributed in India by Penguin Books India,
7th Floor, Infinity Tower – C, DLF Cyber City,
Gurgaon 122002, Haryana

ISBN: 978-178578-603-7

Typeset in Baskerville MT by Marie Doherty

Printed and bound in Great Britain
by Clays Ltd, Elcograf S.p.A.

CONTENTS

For Vanessa, Tanya, Emma, Jodie, Sam and Karen
– the best support squad a woman could have.
With love and heartfelt thanks.

ABOUT THE AUTHOR

Sophie Walker spent twenty years at Reuters as an international journalist and news editor. After a long and trying journey supporting her elder daughter through a diagnosis of autism, she started campaigning for disability rights, particularly those of girls on the autism spectrum, for Ambitious About Autism, Include Me TOO and the National Autistic Society. In 2015, she helped to create the Women's Equality Party, Britain's first feminist political party, which she led and grew into a movement of thousands across the UK. Sophie ran for London Mayor in 2016, and in 2017 stood for election to Westminster, campaigning for equal pay, affordable childcare and an end to violence against women. She was named by *Vogue* in 2018 as one of the 'New Suffragettes' and was dubbed by the *Daily Telegraph* 'this generation's Emmeline Pankhurst'. She is now co-director of Activate Collective, a fund to support female community activists to run for political office, and Chief Executive of Young Women's Trust which campaigns for economic justice for young women. Sophie lives in North London with her husband and four children and is still trying to figure out how to get back to Glasgow, where she grew up.

INTRODUCTION

It's six thirty in the morning. The sky is clear blue, and the air is cool on my face.

I stretch up and down; check my laces; swing my arms once – twice – and set off running. Down the street, around the corner, through the park.

It is a beautiful July morning in London. In my ears, BBC Radio 4 broadcasts news from around the world.

In Helsinki, US President Donald Trump has declared in a news conference with Vladimir Putin that he believes the Russian president over his own intelligence agencies on the issue of Russian interference in the US presidential election.

From Geneva, the United Nations High Commissioner for Refugees is calling for access for aid workers to almost a quarter of a million Syrians stranded with no shelter or food in the desert near Jordan after fleeing a Russian-backed offensive in Deraa, the birthplace of protests in 2011 that sparked this ongoing civil war.

In London, it is announced that the architects of Brexit will be fined for irregularities in financing their part of the campaign that broke Britain in two. The police watchdog meanwhile says the Force's response to rising hate crimes in the wake of the referendum has been inadequate.

British Prime Minister Theresa May, still trying to work out what to do, staggers through Westminster clutching votes to herself like straws. Members of Parliament are to vote on whether to go home early for summer break.

In California, blazes have erupted and are spreading across thousands of acres of land every day, putting the lives of locals and emergency service providers at risk.

It feels as though the whole world is on fire and there's no one to put it out.

Through a series of unexpected events that we'll get to in a bit, on this morning, as I run, I'm the leader of a national political party. It's a new party, with new ideas and a whole lot of brilliant, thoughtful and inspiring campaigns and campaigners. Yet, as I pace past tidy houses on my street, turn right towards the park and cross over still-quiet roads past parked cars, with this dreadful state of affairs ringing in my ears, I feel desperate about my capacity to do anything about any of it. There's just *so much* of it. I wonder how I can keep going in the face of such enormous barriers to a fair and peaceful world. I wonder how I can persuade other people to keep going. I wonder how many people listened to the news this morning and thought that any attempt to change the world was pointless. I wonder how many simply switched it off, or turned to a different station or channel. I wonder how many caring people quailed at that catalogue of sadness and outrage. And I wonder whether anyone, anywhere in the world, has figured out how to keep firefighting when the fires keep breaking out in new places with flames that seem ever hotter and more destructive and smoke that feels like it might choke you.

I inhale lungfuls of fresh air and consider. We need a movement of millions to tackle all of this stuff. We need a plan that's simple and effective and also sustainable, because we're going to have to fight these fires in shifts, over a long period of time. I wonder, what kind of plan would work for that? Wouldn't it need to be vast and involved? Or should it be short and to the point? Would it need to detail practical measures for activism? A strategic approach? Offer powerful inspiration? Or do we essentially need philosophical comforts? And where would I find all of the answers to this? Who should I ask?

I finished that run sure of one thing. We have to make sure the destructive blazes are snuffed out. We have to sow a better world for all of us. We can only do this together. Saving the world has to involve you. Our plan to save the world has to ensure that you can keep going when I'm flagging, and that I can keep going when you're flagging.

At this point you might be undecided about joining the rebellion – or about the need for activism altogether. Perhaps it doesn't seem worth it, given the scale of the problems. Perhaps it seems as though you individually can't make a difference. Maybe you think the change shouldn't start with you but with people in other countries, ones that are doing far worse than us on carbon emissions, or access to education, or human rights. Look, bear with me. Bear with my vision that there can be something better. Consider this suggestion that there is something you can do about the state of the world.

Don't laugh it off.

Don't put this book down!

Whatever you do – don't decide not to care.

Not caring is no way to live.

Not caring leaves the way free for billionaires to bend entire countries to their will. Not caring leaves politics to people whose primary consideration is the desire to protect their own interests. Not caring leaves decision-making to people who lack compassion and imagination.

On 8 November 2016 – the US election day that ushered in the pussy-grabbing, immigrant-denouncing apologist for white nationalism, President Trump – British journalist George Monbiot sent this tweet:

> The choices before the American people are:
> 1. The same old shit
> 2. An entire vat of shit, in which you will drown
> Vote 1. It's all there is.

George was clearly flagging that day. It's a shame, because a lot of people were listening to him. We have to cheer George up. And we have to not be like him in that moment. Because dismissing everything as shit makes you complicit.

Let's instead build something new.

Come with me.

At this point I'd like to take a moment to set out what help this book aims to offer. Key to this activist message is practical support and encouragement: a resource of information for developing the talent you might not yet know you have. But to be clear: this is not a message about fixing yourself first. Because if you're a curious or contemplative person, you've probably tried that, at the urging of other books. You've probably read the ones that say you need to improve yourself before you can improve anything else, and that you need to do that work alone. The guilt and cynicism that those books can foster is stifling. Perhaps you're feeling sceptical now because you feel like you've tried everything already and you're tired of it. That's understandable: a walk into the 'self-help' section of the average bookshop shows tables piled high with lessons for women that they're not good enough – while the philosophy and business sections encourage men to be thoughtful about life without suggesting such levels of inadequacy.

The 'ourselves' in the title of this book is a very deliberate word. This is not a book to tell you and you alone to try harder. I've tried yoga, jogging, eating green, baking and mindfulness. All of those things are good and lovely, and they help build strength and calm, but on their own they are just coping mechanisms for people existing within systems that don't allow them to live freely. The message to 'be your best self' is a deeply cynical one when it is addressed from within an unacknowledged structure of oppression. Eating chia seeds is not going to change the systems that prevent change itself. And it's pointless urging people as individuals simply to try harder when there are centuries of legislative, cultural and economic inequality to overcome. The messages to women, classified as second-class citizens and discriminated against over thousands of years of patriarchy, demonstrate this particularly well: 'Come on, ladies, all you have to do to deal with a sexist workplace is grow a thicker skin!' or 'Come on, ladies, all you have to do to not get raped is to not do anything that might encourage a rapist' or, my personal favourite in terms of sheer absurdity, 'Come on, ladies, all you have to do to get equal pay is learn *how to ask* for a pay rise!'

This book is not going to tell you that the brave new world hinges on you establishing a better work–life balance while maintaining a steady dress size. The brave new world hinges on us shaking off the shackles of despair or anger or hopelessness and making contact with others who are just like us – people who are trying to come up with new ideas and ways of behaving and interacting in order to move our societies, democracies and institutions out of the mud in which so many are floundering. We can only do this work together, and we can only do it if we reach people who have never considered – until now, perhaps – that they might be able to change the world.

We need new activists. We need new campaigners. We need new ideas. We need new spaces for new leaders and new ideas to find one another. We need to think about what leadership is and how more than one person can lead at the same time and how collectively we can inspire each other to step up. We need to make room for people to try and fail and be able to talk about making mistakes or simply wonder aloud for a while what the answers might be.

One of the most important things I learned as an activist (to date; I'm learning new things all the time) is that other people have much, much better ideas than me. I consider that a key part of my work is to:

a. find those people and put them together with more people;

b. absorb those ideas and come up with a plan for how we might make them work in practice; and

c. find more people and more ideas.

Being an activist or a leader is not a job title but an action. One of the most important things I learned as a leader prompted me to step out of that job and write this book: the best way to build power is to give it away. Effective leaders build self-sustaining collectives and movements. They know when to get out of the way for someone with a different perspective and when to hold out a hand and walk forward together with another. Leadership, under the old heroic model, where the masses appoint one man (it's usually a man) to go into battle on behalf of millions, is a crazy and ineffective model whose time is long gone. Yet still we cling to it because human beings are tribal and we believe that our tribal leaders must always be right and certain in all things. And in order for our leaders to be right, someone else has to be wrong. All of that rules out almost immediately any kind of leadership by people brave enough to try new ideas before they've been tested to destruction, or by people brave enough to lead alongside other people with different opinions. And it certainly rules out people who look and sound different, and whose opinions, mannerisms and life experiences are different. People who might need different ways in which to work, grow, learn and maintain the confidence with which to try to change the world.

I never intended to be an activist. I never intended to be a politician. I certainly never intended to be a leader or a (very minor) public figure.

Those things happened because friends and respected colleagues advised and encouraged me, and I listened and I took the hands that were held out to me. They also happened because in the (plentiful) moments when every screaming, frightened nerve told me to stop, I stood up anyway, hands clenched so no one could see me tremble. I've ended up doing what I'm doing because I couldn't *not* do it anymore. When the work is wonderful, I wish everyone could see how wonderful it is and be inspired with me. And when the work is bloody hard, and I don't know how to keep going, I wish everyone who felt like that in the same moment could know that we are all working together, that this is a movement and that we can find support in each other.

One of the questions I often get asked as I go about my work is: 'I want to do something about this. But how can I be brave?' This question appears in letters from thirteen-year-old schoolgirls and is asked at workplace presentations by women in their twenties. Forty-something women ask it at local party branch meetings. Very cool, influential people who I would never have believed could worry about lack of bravery have asked it backstage at events.

My response is this: It is easy to be brave in a world that is built to fit you. Where everything from the height of the handrails on the underground to the temperature of the air conditioning in your office to the pills you take at night for your heart disease are all designed to your physiology. Where the media reflects people who look and sound like you. Where you have sufficient money in your wallet and food in your belly. Where you can move around in the world without fear. Where you know that your voice will be heard. The world is largely not built to fit people who are not male, white, wealthy, straight and non-disabled. The people at the margins of that template live and grow and move and try to thrive despite it. So, if you are asking yourself nervously, 'I want to do something about this. But how can I be brave?', you already are, because you're preparing to make yourself even more uncomfortable in a world that is structured to make sure you always know your place.

I am only brave in the sense that I refuse to know my place. Every time it's suggested to me that I should sit down and be quiet, I get very cross and claustrophobic and refuse, and consequently find myself in all sorts of trouble.

There are many things to feel daunted about when you look at the world. It's not just that so much seems wrong but also the potential personal cost of trying to do something about it. The potential personal impact of trying to intervene is high in our 24-hour media, social media, blogging, Instagramming, digital billboarding, feel-it-with-me world. Who on earth would want to stand up and say, 'Listen to me!' in that hubbub? Who would feel confident of being heard? Who would want to risk looking foolish? Who would want to expose themselves to the tidal wave of trolls ready to take anyone apart who expresses an interest or opinion that differs from theirs? It's entirely natural to want to keep your head down. To curate your social media to show only pictures of shopping and holidays, shared only with family and friends. To stay indoors and surf Netflix instead.

It's so much easier to keep quiet. That's what people with power rely on. They need us to keep quiet and to feel powerless in order to maintain their own power. You not challenging them props them up almost as much as if you were campaigning in support of them.

Don't be daunted. Don't dismiss your power. Fear of being noticed is a fear of being rejected, but guess what? You have already been rejected. The systems that aren't working for you are already dismissing you. You might be ridiculed or disliked by nailing your colours to the post. But the reality is that decisions are being made for and about you every day by people who don't like you or don't see you. Those decisions include *not* making decisions about you – hence the neglect and dismissal you're feeling. So, you might as well be visible.

Different people have different ideas about what makes an activist. I have seen people who seemed to be born to it – who came into the world raging and declaiming, or inquiring and organising, or questioning and persisting. I've heard people say they were born activists, driven to make change for as long as they can remember. Others were convinced as a child that they wanted to make the world a better place. I think those people are brilliant, and quite rare.

We need born activists, but we also need activists who come to it late – the far wider and growing network of people who have for weeks, months and years experienced and observed injustice, double standards, cruelty and hypocrisy … until one day they simply can't put a lid on those experiences and feelings any more, or theorise or drink them away, or numb them in the myriad ways our world beckons us to.

Does that sound like you? I think that you, like the many other people who become activists, have been made into one by the hundreds of incidents that mark you every day, pushing you to conform to a shape that suits society rather than your true self. I think most of us reach a point where we eventually step out of the mould into which our society has pressed us precisely because we are tired of being moulded. I think we become activists because we reach a breaking point. Because we want to smash that mould.

When I was seven years old, my mum gave me a badge that said: 'Girls Are Powerful.' It was a small round button badge with a multicoloured, rocket-shaped font that fizzed and shouted. I remember looking at it and feeling as uncomfortable as I felt thrilled by it. It said out loud something that I'd only ever said inside my head. It made my skin prickle.

I pinned it to my blazer and wore it to school, where the boys in my class took one look and laughed out loud. 'Of course they're not,' sneered one, confident and contemptuous already in his tiny man-skin. I felt furious and hurt that he had squashed something nascent in me and had forced confirmation of something I didn't want to admit to myself just as I had started to rise up against it.

When I was nine years old, I was the monitor for school art class, tasked with helping to prepare for my form's painting sessions. I had to dispense the water pots, bearing faint rainbow rings from earlier sessions, and the paintbrushes, with splayed bristles and peeling wood handles, and plastic trays fitted with discs of watercolour paints. I also had to direct each table monitor to the newspaper pile – fluttery bundles of tabloid pages to be spread across our desks as protection against the mess. Among the pages were photographs of bare-breasted women in small lacey knickers. The boys would roar and point and laugh. The girls would make themselves a bit smaller, huddle over their paintings and make sure not to catch anyone's eye.

When I was eleven years old, there was what used to be called (in the way that public parlance can diminish women's distress) a 'flasher', across the road from the school playground, who called out in a friendly, gentle and persistent way until we came over to the railings. When he had our attention, he exposed himself and became laughingly excited as our realisation and distress grew.

When I was thirteen years old, skinny and gawky and geeky, a boy in my form class said I was disgusting for being so unnaturally tall and unwomanly. He said it to me in form class and said it to me when he passed me in the corridors. He took up a seat behind me in physics class and, winking at the other boys across the room, leaned forward and whispered in my ear when the teacher wasn't looking a stream of contempt for my lack of charm, beauty and curves. After a while he didn't bother whispering anymore but would lean back lazily in his chair and call it over to me without moving his eyes from the blackboard or his workbook. His friends would take up the chant.

When I was fifteen years old, I went through a Goth phase. One night I went to my favourite club wearing a short black skirt and ripped tights. I painted on black eye make-up and crimped my hair. When it was time to leave, I had to wait for ages on the street for a taxi. When I eventually found one, the driver took me home via a long and circuitous route, saying nothing to me as he circled back streets I didn't know and waste ground far from street lights, until I was so frightened that he was looking for a quiet place to attack me that I cried and curled up into a ball on the back seat. Once I was frightened enough, he drove me home and let me out, where under the bathroom light I examined myself, my face and my clothing, and thought I must have brought it on myself.

When I was 21, I visited a boyfriend in the United States who was spending the summer there working. In the Maryland beachside apartment he shared with a group of other male students all working in the local bars and restaurants, I found porn magazines on the Formica kitchen table, peeled back and left open at the money shot – something to be viewed casually over breakfast, perhaps. I reeled back from the pictures, horrified. 'Don't be such a prude,' my boyfriend told me.

I used to argue with that boyfriend and his friends. When I did, they would grin at each other behind my back and call me 'feisty' – a non-threatening version of 'brave', a descriptor for women and animals.

When I was 27 and newly arrived in a journalism job, a senior colleague offered to tell me more about the company over a drink. When we got to the pub, he explained that he could work better with me and do more for my career if I slept with him.

When I was 30, I got pregnant by mistake. My boyfriend and I, knowing each other only a little, nonetheless decided to commit and move in together and look forward to our baby. We both worked for the same company and were both talented and young and ambitious. As the weeks ticked down to my maternity leave, I started to feel very anxious about my future prospects. One day, fretting about the time I would be away from work, I said I wished that we were better able to share parental leave. 'But I don't really need more than two weeks,' the father of my child told me.

When I was 38, divorced and juggling a big work promotion carrying heavy responsibility with single motherhood, my daughter was diagnosed with autism. The process had taken five years. We kept being told that only boys got autism. I expected relief and support after we got the diagnosis, but instead we were sent away to get on with it and denied disability living allowance or special educational needs provision. I changed my work to part-time so that I could support my daughter and do the hours of bureaucratic administration necessary to fight her corner against the authorities. One day – one of many such days – her school rang me to tell me she had lashed out at another pupil. It came to light that the other pupil had been bullying her, one of a ring of persecutors that had ridiculed and threatened her for months on end. 'She brings it on herself,' the school's special educational needs co-ordinator told me, explaining that my daughter's disability made her, as a girl, particularly hard for the other children to deal with. Because girls were supposed to look and play nice.

No single one of these events made me an activist. But the combination of them – and many more – did.

To write this book I interviewed a range of activists up against conditions and challenges very far removed from the struggles of a white Western woman like me. Their stories and experiences are extraordinary in their range and for the grit and determination that these women have consistently shown. I felt inspired and very humbled by what I heard, and I hope that in sharing these thoughts and suggestions with you, we find between us many more new activists to join their efforts. I hope also to show that everyone can be an activist, and that a great many experiences – whether that of a student in Europe protesting the climate crisis or a Syrian campaigner desperately trying to stop the bombing and detention of ordinary people – are linked by a golden thread. Life comes at us thick and fast with injustice, and it won't stop until we each, and together, do something about it.

As feminist activist Julie Bindel put it to me: 'These feelings just chip away at you. I've never known a woman who had a Road to Damascus moment. It's always something that women and girls know – that things aren't fair. And from that it's about opportunity – being in the right place at the right time, being a bit rebellious perhaps – all kinds of things that can be a combination of chance and impetus that then leads you to take on feminism as a priority.'

Imagine finding more ways to create those moments of opportunity, from moments of pain and despair. Imagine finding and giving a voice to all the people currently tussling in still-silent near-mutiny about a whole range of injustices and inequalities. Imagine lifting up all the people who have tried and tried but are finding it so hard to keep going. Imagine bringing together all of those people. Imagine if we all could find each other.

Imagine all of that potential – activating all of the people who are nearly at the tipping point but don't know it yet. Maybe they have been resisting that pull. Maybe they feel that it's too daunting. Or maybe they are ready and have in fact been waiting for *you* all this time. Imagine the impact of inspiring anew the tired but seasoned activist with years of experience and perspective.

This is not a book to teach the technical skills of activism – the practicalities of changing the law, writing policies, mustering social media algorithms for successful campaigns. This is a book that explores how we can maintain energy and determination in the face of enormous barriers, and how we can adopt activism as a philosophy for life, rather than seeing it as a few pitched battles.

I want to challenge the alarming stereotypes of activism that people have raised with me as reasons they couldn't consider themselves campaigners – that it's for adventurers and thrill-seekers, or thick-skinned, seasoned debaters, or a macho band of brothers and just rarely a feisty sister. Together with you, I want to seek out the skills (and awareness of the skills we were born with) needed to create a version of activism that suits us all, inspires us all and sustains us all.

Activism is a rollercoaster. This book plots those downs and ups in a way that will help you to recognise and connect to the feelings you're having, so that you can channel energy from them and nourish and maintain your activism. In the chapters to come, I set out five essential rules of engagement that aim not just to suggest helpful choices but also to show the context in which we make choices and how that context affects our capacity to resist and persist. The five rules are interconnected – embracing one leads you to the next, and the next – in a circle of learning and growing. Because activism isn't a linear journey with a clear starting and stopping point. Activism is a philosophy for life.

To be clear: activism is founded on rebellion. Becoming an activist means rejecting that what we're told is simply the way of things, and instead demanding a better world.

Welcome to the rebellion.

Now let's go and start changing the world.

1 DEFEAT DESPAIR

'You are never stronger than when you land on the other side of despair.'
– Zadie Smith

'It's all a mess. Nobody listens. Me? Nothing I can do. I keep my head down. Live my own life.'

It's a Sunday morning and Tom, aged 28, is buying materials for some weekend DIY. There's a steady stream of people entering and exiting this big suburban store that sells a wide range of home improvement kit and hardware. Outside, the car park is busy with vehicles of all shapes and sizes into which couples, families and weekend workmen load boxes and bags. Inside, the aisles and check-outs are busy with purposeful men and women holding handwritten lists of materials and carrying everything from tins of paint to doorknobs.

But ask them about how they feel about fixing the wider world, and their air of purpose visibly slips.

'Pffft!' Michael, 56, blows out his cheeks, exasperated. I've asked him how he feels about the state of world and whether he might be able to fix that as well as he fixes upholstery. 'I wouldn't know where to start,' he replies. 'And there's no point. Nothing makes a difference, much.'

Sarah, carrying carpet cleaner, agrees. 'Politicians don't care. They're not interested in anyone except themselves,' the 62 year old tells me. 'I'm worried about what kind of world my grandchildren are going to live in, but I don't see that there's much I can do about it except try to look after them myself as best I can.'

Sarah, Michael and Tom's loss of faith is typical of current public attitudes. In 2019 the Ipsos MORI Veracity Index found that politicians were the least-trusted profession surveyed, displacing advertising executives, who most frequently occupied the bottom place. Just 14 per cent of the public said they trusted politicians in general to tell the truth. Separately, research by Young Women's Trust found that 72 per cent of young women aged 18–24 in the UK had less confidence in elected representatives than the previous year. And a poll by PR consultancy firm Edelman found that 60 per cent of Britons believed their views were not represented by British politics.

Americans' trust in US institutions is also in a poor state. A 2018 poll by NPR, PBS NewsHour and Marist showed that Americans have limited confidence in public schools, courts and banks, and even less confidence in big business and politics. Just 8 per cent of those polled had confidence in Congress. Ten per cent trusted the Republican Party and 13 per cent trusted the Democratic Party.

This crisis of democracy is not limited to the West, and it's not new – political trust among current generations has been declining since the 1960s and 70s. In 1974, Takeo Miki became Prime Minister of Japan at a point when the country faced a global post-war recession, unprecedented levels of inflation and a political system rendered ineffective by a lack of collective responsibility. His own ruling Liberal Democratic party was out of policy ideas and dominated by scandals, in-fighting and personal rivalries. At his first press conference, Miki said: 'We face the most difficult situation in the post-war years. The mission of the moment is to restore the people's confidence in politics.'

Fast forward to 2002: Dutch Prime Minister Jan Peter Balkenende was so desperate for a spell to renew public confidence in politics that he based his election campaign imagery on his likeness to Daniel Radcliffe, the actor who portrayed J.K. Rowling's wizard hero Harry Potter. Trust in the national parliament, which had so far held up against a decline in other countries, fell sharply in the Netherlands from 2001, despite the country's high rankings for prosperity and standard of living. Analysis of the fall suggests a rising feeling among voters that the government felt distant and patronising, that there wasn't a chance to make their voices heard in crucial decisions. Globalisation, migration and EU enlargement, against the dissenting voices of anti-Islam and anti-immigrant politicians such as Pim Fortuyn (whose assassination temporarily increased the popularity of his LPF party), all contributed to a rising sense of risk and uncertainty to which voters felt the political establishment was unequal. By 2010, after four coalition cabinets collapsed, Balkenende resigned, having spent his time as prime minister primarily focused on political in-fighting. 'Without trust, any attempt to agree on matters of substance is doomed to failure,' he said.

As Balkenende was stepping down, the new UK Prime Minister David Cameron was pledging to rebuild public trust in politics with the slogan 'We can't go on like this' central to his messaging. He had already declared in his party leadership victory speech of 2005 that he was fed up with the 'name calling, backbiting, point scoring, finger pointing' of Westminster and promised, in a tweet that has now been posted by activists on public billboards across the nation as a post-EU-referendum reproach: 'Britain faces a simple and inescapable choice – stability and strong Government with me, or chaos with [opposition Labour leader] Ed Miliband.'

The swell of distrust has been growing for a long time. Our politicians and political institutions can't say they didn't see it coming. And you don't have to look very far for more reasons why people think leaders and institutions are incapable of action or innovation.

According to a Credit Suisse survey in 2017, 1 per cent of the population own half the world's wealth. The world's 3.5 billion poorest adults each have assets of less than $10,000. Meanwhile, global greenhouse gas emissions have reached record highs, and the Intergovernmental Panel on Climate Change has warned we may only have until 2030 to avert catastrophic climate change. In the Western hemisphere, a decade's worth of austerity budgets – the decision by so many governments to make taxpayers and those dependent on welfare pay for mismanagement of the banks that brought about the financial crisis – has left the most vulnerable on their knees and prey to chancers pretending to be men of the people. Self-styled 'strong men', like US President Donald Trump, Brazilian President Jair Bolsonaro, Hungarian Prime Minister Viktor Orbán and UK politician Nigel Farage, are all hiding their establishment links and spinning tales about immigrants as the real culprits to blame for a widely felt loss of dignity and dependable work.

We're living at a time when populists and politicians are so desperately short of ideas that they have resorted to the oldest strategy in the book: divide and rule. It's a favourite of those with no imagination and a thirst for power. Frighten people and turn them against one another and, with a bit of luck, they won't notice how lacking in true solutions you are. Politics is calcifying because it is dominated by people who look and sound the same: professionalised to death by people who come to it as a paying job rather than to do public service, or who seek a soapbox from which to broadcast their own opinions rather than fresh ideas on behalf of the voting public. The only invention now is the reinvention of angry white men pretending to be prophets of the people, howling about 'identity politics' in what is the most dangerous identity politics of all: the rage of those with power and privilege against any suggestion that it might be time to make room for people who look and sound different.

It is tempting at times like this to look away, to look inward, to protect private spaces and immediate family, as Sarah said at the top of the chapter. It's tempting also to decide that things aren't that bad – to emulate the approach of climate change deniers when it comes to this global political meltdown and tell ourselves that it's just cyclical, it will pass and, really, it's not so serious. Turkish writer Ece Temelkuran, in her book *How to Lose a Country*, describes a London event in 2016, two months after a failed coup in her home country, at which a woman in the audience asked her with pity what help Britain could offer.

Temelkuran writes: 'I pause for a second to unpack the invisible baggage of the question: the fact that she is seeing me as a needy victim; her confidence in her own country's immunity from the political malaise that ruined mine … This is a moment in time when many still believe that Donald Trump cannot be elected, some genuinely hope that the Brexit referendum won't actually mean Britain leaving the European Union, and the majority of Europeans assume that the new leaders of hate are only a passing infatuation.' After a beat, Temelkuran responds to the audience member: 'Whatever happened to Turkey is coming towards you. This political insanity is a global phenomenon. So actually, what can *I* do for you?'

Despair manifests in many different ways. Pretending things are fine while pushing away a worried or sinking feeling is a response that many of us have been trained in. It's often the response to a lifetime of experience that teaches many of us that asking for attention and respect is a dangerous act, that we are not good enough or worthy enough, that we need to work harder and be better to earn significance. It's the same impulse that can also manifest as fierce love and loyalty towards a charismatic snake oil salesman who promises that he sees you and is outraged on your behalf at the way you've been treated.

Despair is seeing the extent of the storm, understanding its ferocity and deciding that your best chance of survival is to hunker down and hope it passes. If you are one of the people in the storm bunker, remember that the people whipping up the tornado are really committed and really busy, and they are not going away. They will relentlessly create a stronger and stronger force for destruction until everything is levelled.

Over the months of writing this book, I have seen and felt the pressure building. News came that Rita Bosaho, Spain's first black female MP, had lost her seat in a general election in which 10 per cent of the Spanish vote was won by the far-right Vox party. Vox attempts to frighten voters into distrusting one another by centring migration as everyone's biggest problem; it also suggests that key to a stable society is rolling back women's rights. Vox wants to scrap legislation to halt violence against women on the grounds that it discriminates against men. The party dehumanises feminists by routinely calling them 'feminazis'.

Bosaho was born in Equatorial Guinea, which has one of the world's worst human rights records. Two of her uncles, as well as other relatives, were killed by the regime that took over when the country gained independence from Spain in 1968. She has lived in Spain since she was four and was working as a nurse's aide at a hospital in Alicante until the financial crisis, when government cuts, combined with a major public spending corruption scandal, prompted her to join the anti-austerity movement and, in turn, Podemos, the left-wing movement that set out to end corruption and achieve social justice.

Speaking to me a few weeks after her election loss, via a journalist friend and translator, Bosaho explains that, while she never needed to be convinced of the importance of activism, she was surprised to find that the crisis created a movement in which her voice could really be heard.

'I was born in a country that has never known what human rights are: a dictatorship. For that reason, I've never had to have a Eureka moment [as regards activism]. But the Indignados movement [a peaceful protest led by ordinary Spaniards who organised sit-ins in city squares against government austerity measures] [...] was like a snowball effect, with more and more people joining in. You could participate in a town square and for the first time your voice could be heard and become important. That had never been possible before in Spain.'

Podemos attracted her because it didn't have the structure of a classic political party, even though she later felt constrained by the structural difficulty of delivering change from within a system designed to encourage stability over revolution. She explains:

'I sometimes get down about the dynamics of how political parties work. At the start everyone wants to change everything, but all of a sudden you are in a political party and that party has to behave within certain structures, and you can't operate in the same way as you do on the street.'

But in the end, Bosaho says: 'I will be an activist until I die. I'll carry on fighting. What motivates me are the roots of my race: over and above being a feminist, I am a black woman. Because of the almost total invisibility of anyone of colour in Spain, my biggest cause is against racism.'

Bosaho may no longer have a seat in Spain's Congress, but her trajectory shows the determination of ordinary people for change. She shows that despair can be overcome – even when progress is not linear. She shows that people do want more than the broken systems they are told to put up with; and they want life to be meaningful and purposeful and rewarding; and they are driven by exasperation at what's on offer instead.

Back at the DIY superstore on my day of informal public polling, I eventually exit towards the car park, where I notice a charity stand has been set up just along from the stacked piles of logs that were rapidly diminishing thanks to the weekend's forecast of a cold snap. Blowing on her fingers in between asking customers to pause for a chat is Milly, a 24-year-old volunteer. She is here to talk to people about the work of an international aid organisation.

'I feel in equal measure dismayed and hopeful,' she tells me. 'We have a lot of barriers, and there's an increasing sense of division that's really vitriolic in the way it's expressed. Everything feels like conflict.'

She continues: 'It's an indictment of where we are that this organisation has to pick up the slack where international governments don't. But I do find hope from the way in which some people rally around this organisation. They don't take the word of states and governments. They do defy the status quo.'

On a cold and drear day, Milly's summing up gives a warm glow. Her words speak of belief in potential action from a group of people who stated that they had given up; she had uncovered the contradiction within all those people repairing and nourishing their homes while despairing over their country. This is the nub of truth from which any activism begins: when you recognise how daunted you are by the world, you are simultaneously recognising that you do want better. Within your despair lies the path out of it. Or, as George Eliot wrote in *Middlemarch*: 'What we call our despair is often only the painful eagerness of unfed hope.'

We should take heart from the words of a woman who had to take a man's name in order to make her voice heard.

Within Eliot's words is another truth that offers us a strategy for casting off despair. Much of the world we live in is structured to foster despair. It's built by the winners, to keep everyone else subdued by feelings of intimidation that they may not even recognise. If despair is structural, so must our response to it be. We can take heart from those who have recognised this before us. The history of activism – and of societal change – is dominated by women building alternative routes, groups and networks when their needs and experiences were ignored or dismissed by those in positions of power. The needs of our communities have long been shored up by local activists striving for practical change and broader solutions when political parties' policies fail.

There are millions of global examples of what former UK Prime Minister David Cameron termed 'Big Society'. This was a campaign that attracted some good campaigning minds but ultimately reeked of political hypocrisy, set as it was against a background of austerity cuts that forced community groups to pick up a very heavy burden as local services were deprived of vital funds. In the end it became a byword for the work of low-paid and unpaid and undervalued people whose lives had not merited investment yet who picked up the pieces of their

broken communities and, with hope, empathy and collaboration, tried to create new solutions.

Their work is where we will start to find the answers
to the enormous questions posed by automation, migration and
the changing nature of work; our global connectivity and the
way we trade; and the conflict and poverty that scars our world
even as we are told we've never had it so good. On-the-ground
activism redraws politics into something much more immediate, real and rooted in people's day-to-day lives. Mass action
movements challenge political certainties. The failed visions
and narrow-minded investment of governments and institutions have fuelled great pain but also channelled protestors'
impatience into finding alternative answers.

Traditional economic and democratic thinking has been
tested to destruction. In this context, activism is not just an
alternative, it's essential.

Jack Monroe's activism began as survival in the most
desperate of circumstances; she lost her job and began a down-
ward spiral into poverty as the welfare state failed to catch her.

'I was an emergency control operator for the fire service.
I was eighteen, living in a rented flat on a decent salary. I had
been training to become a fire fighter, but I got pregnant and
had to cease that immediately. Straight away I began to apply
for other roles within the fire service – jobs that didn't involve
shift work. Throughout my pregnancy and maternity leave, I
applied for jobs – about fifteen different ones. I wasn't given
even an interview for any of them.'

I'm interviewing Monroe in the workspace she has made
at her bungalow home in an Essex town. We sit knee to knee

drinking tea, and when I ask why she thinks this happened, Jack pauses, looks directly at me and says: 'I overheard a senior officer on the telephone saying to someone else: "She fucking chose to have that fucking baby, why is it my responsibility?"'

Monroe returned to work when her son was less than a year old, working consecutive fifteen-hour night shifts, 30 miles from home, and she was often pulled into major incidents that meant she couldn't leave at the end of her shift. A complex rota of friends and her son's father, who also worked shifts, worked to support her and her son, but the stress was unbearable. When her child was eighteen months old, Monroe had a nervous breakdown and resigned from work unable to cope. Friendly senior officers negotiated with other parts of the service to get her job back under conditions that were workable for a young mother, but failed.

Monroe fell instantly into debt. Britain's Department of Work and Pensions ruled that, because she had made herself jobless, she had to wait twelve weeks for any financial support, while the fire service insisted she repay part of her salary. Unable to meet her rent, and with mounting bank charges, she tells me: 'Within six weeks of leaving the fire service I had accrued £3,000 of debt. It took me four years to get out of the hole that decision to resign put me in.'

The room falls very still. She says quietly: 'I felt complete despair. I was daily suicidal. It took a while to get to hungry and desperate – I still had food in my cupboards and things I could sell at that point. But you can only sell your phone once and your camera once and your TV once. And things got worse and worse and worse. I got a temporary job in a coffee

shop for two weeks, passed the trial period and rang the benefits office in delight to say I'd got a job. The very next day the
coffee shop fired me and wouldn't say why. So then the benefits
department decided I had made myself intentionally jobless
again and made me go another six weeks without any pay-
ments. Just at the point I got on my feet I was knocked back off
them. I then sold everything I owned in an open-house sale – I
advertised it on Facebook – every light fitting, child's toy and
piece of clothing – and raised enough money to move house to
somewhere cheaper. Then I was accused by the tax authority
of making a living by selling things from my home.'

For weeks Monroe focused on the survival of her child,
forgoing food regularly in order that he could eat instead;
she switched off heating and hot water in her rented flat and
survived hour to hour freezing cold, hungry and isolated
from friends she was too ashamed to see. Then one day the
local newspaper ran a quote from a local councillor who
said: 'Druggies, drunks and single mums are ruining our high
street.' Monroe was so outraged that she wrote a long letter to the newspaper, which they published in three parts. A
friend said: 'You're good at this. Why don't you write a blog?'
Another friend said: 'I'm doing a charity event where I have
to eat for a pound a day. Given that's what you do, can you
help me?'

Thus was created 'A Girl Called Jack' – familiar now
to many people living in the UK, but for many months an
unknown blog read by tens of people, mainly friends of hers,
appreciative of her articles on the punishing effects of austerity,
interspersed with recipes for those who, like her, were surviving

on food from food banks. Then one day a post called 'Hunger Hurts' went viral. Monroe explains:

'It was a suicide note. The next day I was going to give my son to his father to look after, and then I was going to top myself. I wanted to get all the anger and desperation and fury and sadness and all the lengths I'd been to, and I wanted to get it all down and document it so my life would not have been in vain. [But then] hundreds and hundreds of people got in touch to say they felt the same, or they had felt the same. People offered help. Supermarkets offered food vouchers – that I had to sell on because I didn't have the money to travel to their stores! – and I suddenly felt a lot less alone and a lot less hopeless. It was a feeling of connection that I'd tapped into. Being in poverty is very isolating and lonely, and suddenly there was this whole community of people saying: Hang in there, kid. I suddenly felt like I mattered and what I was saying mattered, and it made a difference.'

She pauses and then smiles. 'That text is now studied in GCSE English language exams, which is bizarre.'

Six months after that blog post, Monroe was interviewed by a national newspaper for a feature on poverty at Christmas. As a sidebar to the piece, she wrote down her week's meals. A major publisher got in touch, saying her ideas could be a helpful resource for other people living through austerity. The book was called *A Girl Called Jack*, and it has sold about 100,000 copies. Jack's latest book, *Tin Can Cook*, aims to support people living on products from food banks to make nourishing meals. It sold 12,000 copies in its first two days of sales, and Monroe donated more than 6,000 copies directly to food banks.

I ask her, considering the road her life has taken, what she thinks it takes to make an activist: what advice she would give to readers wondering if they might or could be one.

'You have to find what drives you,' she says, 'the injustices that make you the most furious; the conversations where someone makes an offhand comment and you know you're going to have to respond. For me, it's food and shelter because I had in the past neither of those things, and the idea that anyone in Britain has an insecure roof over their head and cannot put food on the table makes me burn with despair and anger and injustice.'

As Rita Bosaho and Jack Monroe demonstrate, the moment in which we first act, or take that first step towards becoming an activist, is often stark, defensive and prompted by a painful event that forces us to reconsider how we previously related to the world – and also to the word 'activism' itself.

Chrisann Jarrett is the founder of Let Us Learn, an initiative to help young migrants access higher education. She explains: 'Before I became an activist, I thought it was someone who was quite brave to stand out against something or someone or an institution or an issue that simply didn't sit well with them. I thought it was really synonymous with someone who was bold and spoke out and led something.'

'Now I recognise the desperation to speak out – that you have no choice but to speak out, especially if you yourself were affected by the injustice. I wouldn't see myself as brave. I just didn't have an option. In order to get a solution to the situation that I wanted to resolve, I needed to be that person that stood up to say: I'm affected and so are many others. So, what are we going to do about it?'

Jarrett was born in Jamaica and came to the UK with her family at the age of eight. Her Mum had left ahead of her to study in the UK and had travelled back and forth between the UK and Jamaica to work. Jarrett was looked after by her grandparents, and over that time had built up an image of how her life would be with her mother when she came to the UK.

'It had been unsettling to have her coming and going, and I thought there would be some stability when I came to live in the UK. I thought it was going to be a happy family home, but my Mum had two jobs and she worked so, so hard and wasn't around for the main part. So, I thought, the only way I can impress her and ease her mind would be to do well in my studies because I knew how much education meant to her.'

Jarrett excelled academically, getting good A-level grades and winning a place at the London School of Economics (LSE) to study law. But in the weeks approaching the start of term, while her friends and peers were moving their applications forward with confirmation that they could apply for government-backed student loans, Jarrett received nothing, until a letter came telling her she was ineligible for student finance because she was an international student. The LSE then wrote to tell her that instead of being charged £9,000 a year as a UK student, her tuition fees alone would be £17,000 a year.

The shock was devastating. 'I had worked so hard,' she says. 'I hadn't thought that beyond the school walls were any sort of barriers that would prevent me from reaching where I wanted to reach – let alone my migration story. I'd grown up here since I was eight years old. I didn't think I needed papers to prove I was British.'

Jarrett did not go to university that autumn with her friends. Her mum did not have an answer. They could not pay the fees. Jarrett cried for months. Then one day she heard her mother weeping.

'She was in the kitchen seasoning chicken, and before I walked in I could already hear her sobbing. I'd never heard my mum cry – ever. She'd never shown that much emotion. She was a woman of steel. And now she was saying: "I came to this country because I wanted to be a nurse, but I had too much baggage to be able to do that. I wanted to support my children, and now I feel that you're going to be stopped and I don't want that."'

'I'm telling you: My mum had never cried in front of any of us, and the pain her voice hit me so hard that I thought I had to do something about it.'

Both Chrisann Jarrett and her mother came lawfully to the UK. Her mother fulfilled the necessary administrative paperwork to maintain their lawful status and then in 2007 applied for indefinite leave to remain for herself and her children. By September 2013, when Chrisann was due to start university, the family still hadn't heard back from the Home Office.

'We'd had no paperwork and no communication, but this was usual in our community. We'd heard from so many people that they had submitted their paperwork and not heard back. Then I wrote to ask what was happening, and we got a letter from the Home Office saying they'd lost our paperwork and I was liable to be removed because I had no status. And I was told I had to start all over again to apply for indefinite leave to remain.'

Without British citizenship or indefinite leave to remain in the UK, Jarrett was not eligible for UK student finance terms – neither the lower student fees nor the ability to take out a government student loan.

So she moved to action, first writing a letter to her local newspaper explaining to the public what she was facing, despite having lived in Britain for more than half of her life. Jarrett describes that time as 'like my coming out period of realising that my status differentiated me from my peers. I was coming to terms with the fact that I wasn't British and that I was undocu-mented.' She then began meeting other young people who were also affected, and discovered that 2,000 young migrants every year couldn't take up their university places because of student finance rules that the government had introduced, via secondary legislation, 'so it wasn't even debated on the floor in Parliament', she says.

The LSE wrote to Jarrett and gave her a scholarship. She took up her place but didn't stop the work she'd begun. As she puts it: 'I didn't want to just be the lucky one with 1,999 people left behind that year.'

Jarrett started a project called Let Us Learn, to ask for equal access to higher education for young migrants who call the UK home. By day this young determined woman was studying law at the institution she had only narrowly managed to access, and by night she was working with barristers prepar-ing a Supreme Court case for another young person with a similar profile, who had been born outside the UK, grown up from an early age in the nation, and yet was unable to afford to take up a university place.

'What we did as a campaign was try to collate case studies from young people personally affected, to try to show that this was a systemic issue. The government was saying it wasn't an issue. We argued the problem was that a lot of people only find out their status when they're eighteen years old, and if they don't have what's required it would then take ten years to get either settled status or British citizenship. We argued that's too much obstruction to their education. We argued that you should base it on the fact that they've been here for more than half their life.'

After a year of preparing case studies and witness statements, of meeting and lobbying Members of Parliament and the House of Lords, of talking to the press to raise awareness of the issues, Chrisann Jarrett and her fellow campaigners won a Supreme Court decision that the law was discriminatory and had to be changed. It was.

'That now means that – even though I don't have British citizenship and I don't have indefinite leave to remain yet – because I've lived here for more than half my life and completed my schooling here, and I have three years of lawful residence in the country, I'm able to access student finance,' she explains.

In changing her own life, Jarrett changed the lives and opportunities of thousands more young people.

Both Chrisann Jarrett and Jack Monroe were propelled to action by despair. But they were forged as activists by connecting to the despair of others.

As Monroe puts it: 'Look at how the negative things in the world – Brexit in Britain and Trump's popularity in the United States – have been achieved by drip-feeding information into the public consciousness. Just imagine if there was an equivalent – imagine what the world would look like today if, instead of tapping into people's fears and worst biases and dark thoughts and mobilising them, we could tap into people's possibilities and capabilities and dreams of a better world and harness that instead.'

'We can do that ourselves. All of our actions matter. Contributing even a fraction of karma into a better world helps to create the kind of world we want to see.'

Jack Monroe's inspiring force is most powerful, in my opinion, because it comes from the change she lived through herself. The moment in which she stood face to face with her despair and decided against all the odds to fight for something better is a moment that resonates with something primal in all of us.

As Chrisann Jarrett puts it: 'If we put down our tools now, then who else is going to speak for us?'

We are all living according to an internal, conscious or unconscious decision we've made about how we relate to the world around us and what if any impact we can have on it. A big part of that comes from having absorbed how the world around us makes us feel and modelling that in our own behaviour. So often when we feel despair, we create a personal microclimate that reflects and furthers that feeling of despair. We live just to get through the days. Count down until pay day. Count down until holiday. Count down until retirement.

Decide not to watch or read the news. Avoid people who make us uncomfortable.

Others live in poverty and are consumed each day by dealing with existential basics of hunger, cold and a constant threat of violence. When life involves so much effort not to get hurt, demoralised or damaged, it's easy to believe society's message that those who aren't thriving are themselves at fault. We internalise those messages almost without realising it. And we look to those who seem to exist outside of those criticisms with envy: the rich and the famous, who look golden and carefree. But a public profile and a healthy bank account still don't provide insurance from a culture that finds endless ways to tell us we are no good.

Fearne Cotton is a celebrity: a British television and radio presenter who now presents popular television programmes, following a ten-year run on Britain's top youth radio station, during which she interviewed major music stars. Her career in the public eye meant she was well-known to tabloid newspapers and gossip magazines. Now, after writing a book about the 'harsh and devastating' depression she experienced during that time, she campaigns for honesty about how many of us can succumb to feeling sad and overwhelmed, and seeks to offer a path back to happiness. In her *Happy Place* podcast, she encourages celebrities and campaigners to share the realities of their difficult times and how they have managed to engage positively again with the world.

As Cotton puts it, the turmoil that can grip those with a public profile is a magnified version of the pressures that many other people feel: 'We are indoctrinated to feel we have to keep climbing the ladder to have a bigger version of whoever we are. I didn't see there was any other option. And of course there isn't a linear ascent to glory. You're up and you're down. And when you're down it feels really awful because it's not where you're "supposed" to be.'

We are talking over morning coffee in London. I can't tell whether the pervading sense of calm comes from the fact that we are in a quiet room tucked away from the city's bustle, or because the woman in front of me has been through the mill and come out the other side with composure and warmth and the drive to provide as much solace as possible to others.

'I've been working relentlessly since I was about fifteen,' Cotton begins. 'I didn't really fit into the academic model. I went to a local drama school in the church hall and then got a job presenting a kids' TV show. I got my foot in the door and it stayed in.'

'There was a time in my twenties when I had paparazzi following me everywhere, I was in the papers every day, I was being flown around the world, doing huge entertainment shows. I worked every day, seven days a week. I never had a day off because I didn't see the point. A lot of people in the industry take on the praise and feel elevated. Instead I collected every bit of the bad stuff: the criticism, the jobs you don't get because "you're not right" for this or that; and I carried it around in a backpack with me everywhere.'

'The whole thing affected my self-worth massively, and that's something I've worked on over the last five years. I felt a deep self-loathing and a lack of confidence. I felt very judged and watched because people have judged and watched me from a young age, and that became very heightened. Even now I know that old self-loathing, that comparing yourself to other people. I know there are things that help, and I do things daily that I know will keep me afloat. But some days you can't quite grasp them.'

'Now,' she says, 'I'm very much about connection and conversation. It's been a huge part of my life and my work.'

Fearne Cotton's identification of the link between sad feelings and sad behaviour – that circle of feeling low, tipping into self-criticism and descending into self-loathing – is something that many of us might recognise. It's a pattern that creates its own momentum, where feeling a bit daunted or limited in our choices can lead us to feel even worse about ourselves and our capacity to change the world.

Linked to this is a concept called 'learned helplessness', noted by psychologist Martin Seligman during a series of experiments in the 1960s. (The methods he used in these lab experiments may make you shrink, but bear with me.) In 1965 Seligman researched conditioning, a process by which we learn to associate one thing with another. He would ring a bell and then deliver an electric shock to a dog. Eventually, the dog would hear the bell and react as though it had already been shocked. A little later on, Seligman gave the dog the option to escape the shock. But instead of jumping away from it to another part of the control chamber, the dog instead lay down. Because previous experience had shown the dog that it didn't have control, it felt helpless to avoid a new negative situation.

The inability to control our environment can create a deep and undefeatable depression. It either kills our defiance or leaves us with huge unease each time we attempt to change our circumstances. We receive so many external cues that someone else is in control and it's difficult to understand or accept the extent to which we might have absorbed them. That in turn can lead to a sense that other people *deserve* to be in control, far more so than us. And then it can be very hard to believe that any personal action we might take could be meaningful or effective. One of the clearest examples of this is imposter syndrome, a form of despair many women say they experience. It's demoralising to consider how many brilliant women go about the world feeling massively anxious that they are about to be unveiled as a fraud. But as journalist Yomi Adegoke puts it: 'It is crucial to remember that women are not born feeling less-than. But if you are continually treated as though you are, you eventually internalise it. And this is not merely a synonym for low confidence – imposter syndrome is the logical outcome of a world that was never designed for women to be successful.'

Writing in the *Guardian*, Adegoke says: 'It is time we stopped seeing the problem as being women's refusal to believe in themselves and rather a world that actively refuses to believe in women.'

A first approach to activism and rebellion is to recognise the external factors that have led so many of us to feel so bad and so helpless about ourselves. Working on feeling better isn't about mind over matter or accepting our complicity in our mental ill-health; it's about deciding to behave as though something different is possible – or at least trying to. Being realistic here: failure is part of learning, and no one is going to feel better by berating themselves at the end of a long and difficult day for not being more positive. But we do have to make the vital leap of faith, deciding to behave according to how we wish the world were, rather than how it is now. It's a leap away from the darkness of despair into the unknown.

Transgender rights activist Paris Lees puts it another way: 'If the world makes it absolutely impossible for you to be yourself in the world, you have two options: you can either change yourself or you can change the world.'

Lees began her ten-year journey into activism at the point when she was considering what she saw as a third option: suicide. Born into a working-class family in Nottingham, England, she had endured intense bullying, abuse and a spell in prison by the age of eighteen. But, she tells me, her lowest point, as she stopped identifying as a gay man and started to identify as female, came when she read a national newspaper article by Germaine Greer, written in response to the sex testing of athlete Caster Semenya, that referred to trans women's appearance as a 'ghastly parody'.

Lees explains: 'My existence at that point was completely insupportable. I was experiencing family rejection, I was getting abused in the street, I'd been messed around by the NHS, and people in the media were saying horrible, horrible things about people like me that I knew weren't true, and there was nobody to respond. I reasoned that if the rest of my life was going to be as it was then, I didn't want to live it.'

She was saved by the emergence of a 'burning sense of injustice' that she channelled into journalism in order to present an alternative viewpoint on trans issues. Lees has since featured highly on media lists of influential LGBT+ people and was the first trans woman to write for *Vogue*, voice mainstream radio and present television media shows.

'It has given me huge meaning in my life to feel part of something that's bigger than me,' she says now. 'I think that living a life that's meaningful is really important. I'll always be a campaigner in one sense. I don't want to spend the next ten years of my life in the way I spent my twenties. I want to be a writer. I want to have a happy life. Isn't that the point of activism? That we get to be happy and live a full and meaningful life?'

Living the life you want while working on the world so that it catches up is also known as the 'politics of prefiguration'. Setting off on a journey to a better world doesn't necessarily mean you will see it. But by being on that journey you can start to live in a way that reflects the world you want to see. Things can start to change when people declare their intention to change them. If you embody what you aspire to – even if all you know to begin with is that you want something different – you are already making a change.

A good example of this is the Occupy movement. It's sometimes held up as an example of a campaign that fizzled out because it didn't have a single unified demand or a clear roadmap for like-minded protestors who wanted to grow the movement. (And thus it provides a valuable lesson for future activists.) But it had an incredibly punchy starting point: opposed to social and economic inequality and the power of large corporations and finance, it asked people to take a close look at why, who and what was encouraging them to focus so closely on personal (un)happiness. In order to persuade people to defeat despair and get campaigning, Occupy understood the essential first consideration: understanding context. And that was the capitalist, corporate, individualistic society that bashes us all over the head every day with millions of messages about whether we are good enough, then feeds off our resulting unhappiness to con us into thinking that buying, instead of being, can resolve our woe.

Occupy believed that its movement could prefigure a better society in the future by doing away with hierarchies and societal structures, and thus enabling people to see a different kind of life could be possible. That's an exceptionally hard task these days now that 'fake news' has become an additional tool of politicians and populists. They have created, via bots and misinformation, an additional infrastructure of deception to tell us that our pain, poverty and fear is not real. That none of this is actually happening. That they didn't actually say what they said yesterday, while they take our rights away.

Viktor Frankl was a professor of neurology and psychiatry at the University of Vienna Medical School. During the Second World War he spent three years in Auschwitz, Dachau and other concentration camps. In his book *Man's Search for Meaning*, he writes about the experience of having *everything* taken away from him, whether possessions or values, human rights or the right to speak. He writes of living in extreme pain, hunger and cold; and of how, amid the horror of that experience, he found ways and reasons to live. Frankl writes about how human beings can detach their minds from terrible living conditions as a form of self-defence, yet through this act can discover an essential truth: that everything can be taken from a person but the freedom to choose one's attitude in any given set of circumstances. To choose one's own way.

As he unveils this marvellous liberation to us, Frankl, who died in 1997, the author of 32 books, also reveals the pain it brings. A person's search for meaning is likely to create inner tension rather than equilibrium. But Frankl maintains that this tension is an important part of mental health, for to question is to remain engaged with the world.

We have to change the way we engage with it, starting with how we think about the world and our place in it. What if the next step on this thought journey wasn't 'What do I need to change about myself to be happy?' but 'How can I live differently? What kind of world do I want to live in? How does the wellbeing of others affect me?'

Seligman, who went on to write a number of books about understanding happiness, suggested a solution to the tension Frankl writes about. He posits that, ultimately, meaning comes from serving something beyond yourself and, in so doing, developing the best within you. He advises: 'Use your signature strengths and virtues in the service of something much larger than you are.'

A 'signature strength' sounds off-putting, I think. But if we consider it less as a specialist skill and more as something that you have personally acquired through years of being yourself, then it becomes more accessible. For example, I am very impatient and argumentative. These are not personal attributes that I'm particularly proud of, but they do help to make me an effective activist. Alongside that, I have accumulated years of experience as a carer to a child with special educational needs.

That gives me a particular perspective and the kind of know-ledge of the UK education and healthcare systems that only a particular group of people living with disability or caring for people with disability would know about. So, if you are reading this wondering how to accrue a signature strength, don't worry. You already have it, or your passion will lead you to develop it. Maybe your friends have been too polite to point it out. What you may feel embarrassed about as personality faults at home might be very effective in activist circles. Your awkwardness and difference, your lived experience – put them together with a curiosity about how your experience compares to that of other people and you are on your way.

You might have been holding off in the hope that some-where, somehow, someone was coming to the rescue. No one is coming to the rescue. Get that fantasy out of the way and the mists clear. The fact that nobody is coming to the rescue means one thing. It's up to you now to save yourself.

Welcome to your liberation.

You can act to save yourself and others by asking ques-tions rather than feeling you have to have all the answers – or blusteringly pretending you do. We'd get further faster if more people admitted they don't know the answers to some of the toughest questions. There has never been such a limited range of political ideas as on offer right now. (I don't mean available – wonderful and creative minds suggest new routes almost daily. I'm talking about the tediously predictable segmentation of the main political parties and positions.) That thought that's been knocking around inside your head – you know, the one that you can't ignore any more, the one that prompted you to pick this book up – it could be the breakthrough we've all been waiting for.

And in the meantime, the will to demand something radically different, even if you may not yet know what this is, will do to start. We're in a good place to demand something radically different. As Mary Shelley put it, invention is created out of chaos. We certainly have no shortage of chaos.

Let's come back to despair for just a moment.

The thing about despair is that you will visit it again. Although this book lays out five rules for rebellion, they will not take you on a one-way journey. You'll revisit some stages multiple times; you may loop back on yourself, or at times feel cut off from the point you're trying to reach. I decided to write this book after quitting a job to which I was intensely emotionally attached and in which I felt great pride. But after four years, I felt that I wasn't making enough progress and that if I really wanted to make a difference, then I had to stop and rethink and try a different approach. I felt despair in that moment. I felt that I had lost my vision, that my early ideals had been compromised. I felt exposed in admitting my mistakes. I felt like I was breaking a promise I had made to others. But all I knew was that I had to stop in order to continue another way.

Landing in despair happens. But each time you leave it, you are recommitting to claiming creativity from chaos and darkness; that will lead you on to better things.

Simone de Beauvoir said that it is in the knowledge of the genuine conditions of our lives that we must draw our strength to live and our reasons for living. My personal translation of this is that it's really hard work being an activist. It requires a lot of dedication and patience. It requires having one conversation after another after another, in order to inch forward. It's not enough to be committed yourself and to meet other people who are already on board. You have to reach out to new people, again and again; support them when they are tired; re-connect again and again to other local activists and causes. You have to keep building.

Being an activist requires a determination to step out of despair. Congratulations. You're already there.

2 CHANNEL RAGE

*'Angry women care. Angry women speak and
yell and sob their truths.'*
– Lyz Lenz

'They say depression is "frozen anger", which is something I've
experienced over the last few years. But anger beats the hell out
of depression because anger means the problem isn't me. It's
out there. And if it's out there, there's an injustice happening,
a problem that needs addressing.'

Athena Stevens is an actor, writer and director. She burns
with the injustice of the world. Her work glows with it. I've
watched performances of hers that left my skin tingling and
reinforced my resolve like steel. Stevens was the first person
I thought of as someone who could teach us how to channel
our rage. So I was surprised to hear the disappointment in her
initial response to my invitation.

'There was about a quarter of my heart that went "NO!
I'm not an angry person. I'm not. I'm NOT! Why can't Sophie

present me as a grieving activist? It'd be so much more roman-tic."' This response, Stevens explains, was driven by worry that her contribution would be diminished by being characterised as angry.

'We are so quick to dismiss people by saying "they're just angry" or "anger is not productive" or "people should embrace peace and not anger" that it leads to contempt and ultimately shutting people down. So being known as "angry" scares me, and in the wrong hands, that word really hurts.'

'And yet, anger is sometimes the only healthy response to the injustice of this world.'

Moving into a philosophy of activism means allowing your despair to thaw. The process of thawing out what has kept you immobile can at first bring extreme emotional and physical dis-comfort and often real, raw pain. Your anger might take your breath away. It might make you grind your teeth. When you engage with the subject that is the focus of your activist intent, your stomach might hurt or your throat tighten. Recognising these symptoms as anger means you can start to redirect it out of your body and towards the source. It might take some time. And it might involve talking to people, casually or in a support group or other therapy.

I didn't fully realise at first that the compulsion I discovered a decade ago to run long distance races – which involved com-mitted, hours-long training programmes – was a first attempt to manage and work through the anger that had built up over years of unhappiness and difficulty. There were times, running along solitary country tracks in wind, rain, snow, mud or bak-ing heat that I would weep and roar and laugh hysterically and then weep again. My feet were taking me on one journey, while my mind took me on another, from depression and anxiety to relief and an understanding of the source of that rage. Now, as well as running, I see a counsellor regularly to work through those feelings. I consider it vital work to establish a respectful and safe relationship with my anger. This exploration of my anger helps me to recognise the layers of it that have accumulated over my life and to track its sources – to come to terms with some, and to recognise that others require a campaign. There are times when my anger, and the anxiety via which it so often manifests, feels like a life sentence. There are times when I feel that I personally am the problem. When that happens, I remind myself of the words of Simone Weil, French philosopher and political activist, who said blame is the attribution of pain somewhere else. So long as you are blaming yourself, you are directing your anger to the wrong place.

The price of that misdirection is very high. In her book, *Anger Is Your Ally*, therapist Bina Breitner writes that, if you ignore your anger, 'You're generating physical distress, discounting yourself and blaming the wrong person – you. You also have to keep dealing with the consequences of whatever is making you angry: because you aren't fully informed about what's going on, you're unable to protect yourself. And you're living without an important part of yourself present.'

The idea that an important part of yourself might be a hot rage is quite an alarming one. But is it not more alarming to contemplate living a half-life, sealed off from bits of yourself that rumble mutinously and perpetually? Is it not more disquieting to consider what energy you could unleash and what answers you might find if you accepted that part of yourself?

Breitner urges: 'When you listen to and collaborate with your anger in your own self-interest, you shift from being reactive (that flood of anger) to being proactive. It takes practice. Most of us are more accustomed to paying this kind of attention to another person than we are to ourselves. But please recall that anger comes from your deep self. It's talking to you, it never lies, it has important information for you, and that information is protective. It exists to care about you for your entire life, and it's always on your side.'

Nimko Ali is a Somali activist working to end female genital mutilation (FGM). She describes herself as an unintentional activist driven by what happened to her, proactive for a cause that seeks to ensure no other young girl endures what she did. I've seen Ali in action, and she is as targeted and driven as a heat-seeking missile.

When I ask her whether she calls herself an activist, she responds: 'I'm a trouble-maker. My life was shaken for no reason. Had I not had FGM and seen civil war, I'd be a different person. All the things that happened to me were unnecessary. I want to give people nightmares so that they are appreciative of the good things.'

I've heard Ali talk about her life in many different settings, from community centres to political rallies. But each time we sit down to consider the events that led to her current work, I am struck by her frankness, her rage, her strategic nous and her sense of humour. It is a potent character combination that enables her, both in our conversations and in those she has daily with major decision-makers, to summarise simultaneously the awfulness of undergoing FGM, the ineptitude of public servants who had the job of protecting her and the drive that both those things awoke in her to change lives by changing attitudes.

'I was seven when I had FGM,' Ali recalls. 'I understood afterwards that my mother wouldn't talk about it, and I was angry. I expected her to apologise to me for this horrible thing, and that never came. I talked to my teacher about it, and she said, "Oh, well. That's what happens to girls like you." When I was eleven, I collapsed in the playground when my kidneys almost failed, and I woke up hoping someone would ask me if I was okay and instead saw a nurse smiling at me. I thought: What on earth is there to be smiling about?'

It wasn't until she was 27 that Ali came out as an FGM survivor. She had joined a feminist network in Bristol, where she became resident after her family escaped the war in Hargeisa, and she was asked to talk to a group of young Somalian girls. Entering the room, she was faced with a confident and streetwise bunch. When one of them wisecracked, 'Is FGM Halal?', Ali, horrified, asked the room what they could possibly know about FGM. 'I said, "Have any of you even had it?" I thought they were being flippant and couldn't know anything about something so horrific. Of the fourteen girls in the room, thirteen put their hands up. Then I thought, My God, I have a responsibility to do something about this.'

Nimko Ali co-founded the charity Daughters of Eve and headed to Whitehall. 'Nobody knows how powerful they really are as individuals to lobby people in power. The first thing I did was write to the Home Office and say, "Can I talk to you about protecting girls from FGM in the UK?" I wanted criminal legislation. I was the perfect activist: I understood power and process. I didn't look too threatening. I had humour. And early trauma.'

Ali set herself the task of ending FGM by 2030. She has lobbied and worked with politicians right across the spectrum. In November 2018 the British government pledged £50 million to attempt to end FGM by that same date, announcing that the money would go to grassroots programmes led by African women in their own communities and countries – a point about funding frontline activists that Ali has long been insistent on. Now she has set up global charity The Five Foundation, based on the UN's fifth global goal of gender equality, to dramatically increase funding to such projects.

Talking to her, it's clear Ali has channelled her frustration and pain into positive impact. What upsets her now, she says, is wasted opportunity.

'The foundations of this wave of activism were laid with the first dial-up generation, when you had information at your fingertips but it wasn't in your face all the time. When people finally saw the world in one picture rather than through other people's narratives. There was more equality and integration. It felt like there was a levelling. And all that has fallen apart because the generation above us hasn't grown up. People are getting more and more tribal. I've seen what tribal politics does, when I grew up in Somaliland, where the war happened. Extremes freak me out.'

As Nimko Ali makes clear, freeing your anger is only the first step. Next comes the task of working out how to express it – and how to be meaningfully heard – in an environment where others have chosen other survival methods. Often our first attempt to speak out runs into the brick wall of those who choose to deny our anger as a means of protecting themselves from the truth. Anger gets a bad rap because it destabilises the status quo. And there are so very many people protecting the status quo.

Athena Stevens writes to me: 'When I think about the over-arching thing that creates a huge amount of trauma and pain in the world, wilful blindness is the single biggest force and the thing that holds progress back. We all think we are a force for good in this world, but that can result in not seeing ourselves and others complexly. Weinstein thought he was a feminist. The Labour Party thinks they are "for the many". Everyone thinks they are on the side of disability rights. Statistically speaking, that's not possible. If that was the case, we'd be *way* further along by now.'

'Instead, what is more likely to happen when you con-front people about the way they contribute to injustice is they start to feel threatened – "I'm not racist, I have black friends." "You can call me out but I don't believe conflict solves anything because I'm a peaceful person." "The work that needs to be done is over there – I don't need to change, I'm not part of the problem."'

And once a decision has been made that you're not the problem, you don't have to act. And when you don't have to act, you're free to judge. And when you're free to judge, then the first thing you judge is the people doing the work who sud-denly look a little extreme, or aggressive or angry.

'We judge and come up with reasons as to why this time the fight for justice is too extreme,' Stevens says. 'It's not going to work. It's not what we would do. We wouldn't be that confrontational.'

She directs me to Martin Luther King Jr's 'Letter from Birmingham Jail', in which she says she first recognised her own frustration. King writes that he has realised that the biggest barrier to Black rights 'is not the White Citizen's Counciler or the Ku Klux Klanner, but the white moderate, who is more devoted to "order" than to justice; who prefers a negative peace which is the absence of tension to a positive peace which is the presence of justice; who constantly says: "I agree with you in the goal you seek, but I cannot agree with your methods of direct action"; who paternalistically believes he can set the timetable for another man's freedom; who lives by a mythical concept of time and who constantly advises the Negro to wait for a "more convenient season". Shallow understanding from people of good will is more frustrating than absolute misunderstanding from people of ill will. Lukewarm acceptance is much more bewildering than outright rejection.'

It is not a surprise, then, to see the anger of those who have faced their pain and inequality increasingly spill on to the streets. At the time of writing this chapter, Hong Kong has seen its biggest protests in nearly a decade, with more than a million people protesting a plan by authorities to allow extradition to China – they're taking to the streets to march, halt traffic and face down violent counter-protestors while police use tear gas and rubber bullets against them. In Britain, London and other big cities have been destabilised by Extinction Rebellion (XR) activists, whose fury and fear for the future have been channelled into mass action.

On a rainy Wednesday in June, I'm sitting in a café with Laura Krarup Frandsen. A young fashion design student, she is carefully choosing her words as she tells me about her activist awakening.

Born in a small town in Denmark, Frandsen came to London to study an MA in fashion. But the decision to take up her place had come only after months of struggling with an awakening about the climate crisis, and the fashion industry's role within it in particular.

'Between applying for and being offered the place, I had started to change my perception of the industry. I had become more aware. I was looking at my own consumer habits. I started to realise that I didn't feel good about buying clothes anymore. I started feeling physically ill and sick when I walked into fashion shops. It made me feel really awful,' she tells me.

Frandsen took the decision to attend the course, but her depression mounted. 'I felt I was really alone in this feeling of knowing that the world is breaking down. I felt like I was in this fashion bubble and no one was freaking out. It made me feel either that I was completely overreacting or the whole world was insane. Eventually, I had to make the decision to take a year out.'

During this time, Frandsen noticed the work of Extinction Rebellion, which in November 2018 brought much of central London to a standstill with mass demonstrations that blocked five of the city's main bridges to protest government inaction on climate breakdown. As part of a wide-ranging series of

civil disobedience protests aimed at forcing emergency environmental action from political leaders, activists formed human
chains to close roads, glued themselves to buildings, organised
mass bike rides and sit-ins on major traffic intersections, and
announced plans to disrupt flights from Heathrow during its
busiest summer season. Many dozens were arrested over the
course of these multiple events, including Frandsen.

'I had so much anger and anxiety built up in me. I reached
out to a local meeting of a newly set-up XR group. I didn't
know anyone, but finding the group was such a relief. I found a
whole group of people who had all the same feelings and were
saying all the same things that I'd been screaming about for two
years but had felt alone and like an idiot, irrelevant,' she says.

Laura Krarup Frandsen chose not to create a final collection for her fashion course. Instead she staged a 'die-in' at her
graduate show, simulating a mass death with other activists to
launch Extinction Rebellion's #BoycottFashion campaign that
urged supporters to disrupt the fashion industry by refusing to
buy new clothing or materials for a year. With the current pace
of ecological breakdown and its impact on food production,
the fashion industry's use of land to grow cotton and its forecast production growth in coming decades was something no
sustainable fashion collection could offset, she decided.

'There is a massive need for people who are able to be
frank and open and do some kind of damage control, so we
don't just go on like this. I want to provoke my peers to think
differently. When the problem is that we're consuming this
planet to death, it's not really solving anything to replace one
fibre with another, or replace chemicals with natural dyes. The

problem is our consumption. If we continue like that, we have lost the battle.'

Watching this clear-eyed and resolute young woman, I am struck and inspired. She does not look like the typical depiction of an angry woman. (More of this very shortly.) But recognising and embracing her anger was vital to overcoming her grief and paralysis, Frandsen says.

'I think we have to react to the anger that we're feeling. I started to feel really angry when I realised – looking to the leaders, looking to the government, to the people who are supposed to do what's in the interest and safety of the public, that they're not doing that. I don't think you can not feel angry when you realise that. The fear and despair and the feeling of complete hopelessness comes first. And then you get really angry. It takes for people to have that realisation to get angry – the realisation that we are not being protected, that the government is not doing what's necessary to prevent unthinkable disaster. It takes that realisation to act on it.'

'As a public we are not angry enough. As activists we are using our anger as fuel.'

The idea of anger as fuel, as a way to set light to structures that are not paying attention, is compelling. And as Laura Krarup Frandsen and Extinction Rebellion have shown, it's effective. But for women as individuals there is often a cost to expressing anger at our lack of representation. It's the dismissal of our anger precisely because it is female rage.

How many women have been told by men they do not know to smile, to 'cheer up, love', simply because our going-about-the-day face was not expressing placatory contentment?

How deep runs the expectation, cultivated by millennia of male power, that women are decorative, primed to obey, care, gratify and submit? You can see how deep it runs the moment that we override the master switch. A woman's anger provokes indignation, fear, disbelief and extreme aggression. Our female anger is questioned again and again and again. We are dismissed, laughed at, threatened.

I remember one day nearly eighteen years ago when I took my brand-new baby girl out in her pram. The pram was an old-fashioned carrier, with big shiny wheels and a grand hood. Grace was born in the winter. The weather was bitterly cold. I didn't want to take her out, but I was desperate to escape the house and decided I would walk around the block. I was still healing from a Caesarean section. I walked very slowly up the high street near my home. My baby was silent, shocked into sleep perhaps by the extreme cold air against the tiny sliver of her cheek – the only skin exposed between snug woollen hat and blankets that swaddled her body.

About halfway up the street, a car had pulled across the pavement. Its driver had bounced it over the kerb and got out to chat with a friend in the doorway of a small shop. As they exchanged lazy dialogue, both men watched my slow approach. I drew near, and it became clear that there was not enough space for me to push my pram through the gap left on the pavement. I would either have to push the pram off the kerb, around the car into oncoming traffic and then back up onto the kerb, or ask the driver to move his car. I hesitated, hoping he would see my predicament and act. Instead he watched me hesitate. So, I asked him if he could please move his car. 'You'll have to go round, love,' was the reply. I pointed out that I would have to push my pram into the traffic and asked him again to please move his car back a little. 'I'm talking to my friend,' came the reply, terse now.

In retrospect the terseness was a warning, but in my painful, post-surgery, sleep-deprived haze, I didn't hear it. I was angry with him. And so, I said, this time angrily, 'I've got a baby here, and you're being unreasonable. Please move your car off the pavement.'

I remember that man's answer like it was yesterday. His face transformed in fury and he became dog-like as he snarled and his eyes reduced to slits; he lunged at me and roared: 'Don't you FUCKING tell me what to do, you CUNT.'

Charlotte Wood, author of *The Natural Way of Things*, a novel that concerns the punishment of young women who speak out about mistreatment, wrote a piece in the *Guardian* sixteen years after this incident that I discovered only recently. It made me reflect on how little has changed. She wrote: 'When people talk to me about misogyny, the A-word always comes up. Journalists ask it earnestly, almost sadly, and so do readers: "Are you angry?" I feel as if I'm supposed to say no, that saying yes will somehow let the side down, get us all in trouble.'

When Wood's article was published, I had become the leader of a political party. We started the party in 2015, an attempt by a collective of women and some men to drive a feminist agenda into the heart of politics by creating Britain's first feminist political party. I joined the group of activists building the Women's Equality Party with no hope or expectation beyond being a part of the change I wanted to see. We were fed up at the glacial pace of change and the complacency of other political parties towards women. I did not expect to become a public figure, nor did I put myself forward for the leadership position. However, a group of my peers asked me if I would provide a face and voice to the work we were all doing while we got the mission off the ground, and – after a long weekend of walking up and down my kitchen and discussing with my family how we would handle the personal and financial impact of me stepping away from my job – I agreed.

While I was learning the job of being a feminist political leader, the American cable television network HBO screened its reboot of *Westworld*, the science fiction story of an ultra-high-tech theme park where the grotesquely wealthy, predominantly male tourists act out and pursue their ultimate fantasies upon a cast of stunningly lifelike robot hosts. Violent and degrading storylines abound in which women particularly are abused and humiliated. But then the robots fight back. Standout cast members Thandie Newton and Evan Rachel Wood play androids programmed to be a brothel madam and a farmer's daughter, whose journey into vengeful sentience dumbfounds and horrifies their male masters, from Westworld engineers to holidaymakers. The series became the most-watched first season of any HBO original series and lit discussions across social media for months.

It felt like a horribly apt backdrop to some of the experiences I was having as I went out to discuss with the public and the media why I felt politics needed a feminist reboot to consider the lives and needs of the half of the population that had been cast as props in the lives of the other half. What became clear to me very quickly was that any anger on my part would not be tolerated – even as every discussion was specifically shaped to provoke and belittle me. Interviews would routinely start with the question: 'Haven't women got enough equality?' I would go from television studio to radio station to make what I thought were important and valid points about the injustice and inequality experienced by women; I would often have to make them against furiously outraged men; and yet I was the one who 'lost' if I expressed the tiniest suggestion of frustration. Again and again I was invited to debate misogynist trolls making a career out of sexism, but the emphasis would be on whether I could keep calm both during the event and afterwards, when my words, expression and appearance would be taken apart on social media, often by prominent men with millions of followers, and then digested further in subterranean chatrooms for men's rights activists.

When #MeToo, the social media movement against women's sexual harassment, burst onto the scene, I was regularly asked to discuss violence against women and girls, but in terms that insisted I could only discuss it if I agreed first which kinds of violence against women didn't matter. Again and again I would try to persuade my interlocutors to understand that violence was a spectrum, with harassment in one place and rape in another; and that we could only tackle both when we took both seriously. I was dismissed by one talk show host as a 'stupid woman' mid-sentence, on air, while others wanted to know specifically what sexual harassment I had experienced and how much detail I was prepared to go into. My interviewers would lean forward, eyes alight, and we all knew this was the deal, the

bargaining chip to get my small political party and its policies
a brief four minutes of national coverage, if only I would put
out for them as it were, with private stories of pain and humilia-
tion. I had to talk about the sexual revolution that women were
bringing in terms of where I personally had been touched and
how I had felt about it. Write an article for us, other editors
would ask. Start by saying how tainted and humiliated you felt.

As a young woman I had been used to being dismissed
by bantering manboys of my acquaintance as feisty, spiky
and argumentative because I frequently asked questions or
presented an alternative view. But this time I was up against
media and tech machines built and dominated by men using
those structures to perpetuate their own narrative and power.
I was up against big businesses run by men. (At the time of
writing the six female CEOs of FTSE 100 firms are not only
outnumbered by men but by men called Steve.) I was up against
platforms run by the likes of Twitter boss Jack Dorsey – a white,
straight, non-disabled rich man who has confessed that he
simply didn't anticipate the level of abuse and harassment his
platform enables. I ran a lot to work off the stress. When that
didn't work, I smoked and I drank. And when that didn't work,
I would often cry – bitter tears of rage – at the pantomime I
had to endure in order to keep building this movement and
express the dire urgency of achieving women's liberation.

'If men knew how often women were filled with white-hot
rage when we cried, they would be staggered,' says Soraya
Chemaly in her book *Rage Becomes Her*. Chemaly spells out
clearly the extent of the media's power in squashing and ridi-
culing or simply ignoring women's anger.

'Women make up fewer than 27 per cent of senior media management positions and only one third of newsroom managers. Among the top hundred global media companies, men make up 80 per cent of directors. Studies of other media such as movies, television, gaming and pornography, as well as tech, mirror these numbers.' And, she adds: 'Offline status quo imbalances have migrated online, where they take on even greater power and scope.'

Chemaly's point – as industry analysts also persistently point out – is that when social media companies such as Facebook and Twitter 'verify', or authenticate users online on the basis of their public profiles, they give well-known individuals and companies already operating at the top of hierarchies another boost up. That amplifies already more powerful voices by establishing them online with higher visibility, security, marketing advantages and prominence.

In this context, Chemaly goes on to say, anger is a moral obligation for women, the urgency of which is thrown into sharp relief by consideration of our other priorities.

'Anger is a moral emotion that hinges on our making judgments about the people and the world around us. As women, we are supposed to be one step removed from both moral thinking and the authority that comes with it. Our feelings of anger, deep in our bones, our blood and our minds, are a refutation of that oppressive standard and the control of women that comes with it. It is not only that we have the right to claim anger. It is that our anger is a moral obligation. If we are willing to spend time, money and effort for so many other things, surely liberating our anger should make the cut.'

I wish now that I had expressed more of my anger. I wish I had not submitted to the insistence of media men, and the socialised response that gripped me as it grips so many of us – the powerful behavioural response to be polite in the face of those building and manning the scaffolding and ramparts of patriarchy. I wish that more female activists were able to let themselves feel the same anger as second-wave feminists did. It has been wonderful to see a new generation of women assert themselves as feminists, regardless of the toxicity of the word to so many. But we need many more female activists to consciously reject those decades of attempts to rebrand feminism as something no right-minded person would want to associate with, and also, simultaneously, to reject the accompanying fear of being seen as furious by those seeking to belittle feminism. I want more women to feel their anger and let it flow.

The original second-wave texts were full of that fury. As a teenager reading Betty Friedan's *The Feminine Mystique*, I was rocked by her description of the paralysis of the suburban wife. (Imagine if I had known then the paralysis of the polite female politician!) Friedan described the mute anger so many women held: 'Each suburban wife struggles with it alone. As she made the beds, shopped for groceries, matched slipcover material, ate peanut butter sandwiches with her children, chauffeured Cub Scouts and Brownies, lay beside her husband at night – she was afraid to ask even of herself the silent question – "Is this all?"'

Friedan continues later in the book: 'It is not possible to preserve one's identity by adjusting for any length of time to a frame of reference that is in itself destructive to it. It is very hard indeed for a human being to sustain such an "inner" split

– conforming outwardly to one reality, while trying to maintain inwardly the value it deserves.'

In this context, the expression of anger is the only way that a woman can fully become a person. As Friedan concludes: 'Who knows what women can be when they are finally free to become themselves?'

The last quote weighs heavy with irony given Friedan's unwillingness to engage with lesbian activism. As one of the founders of the National Organisation for Women (NOW), she coined the phrase the 'lavender menace' to describe what she saw as a side issue for feminists that would undermine the cause of women's liberation.

We can recognise the momentum created by Friedan's anger while recognising the limits of her understanding about different female experiences – likewise the shortfall between energy and representation that often marked the recent marches and social media movements protesting Trump's election win and his assault on women's rights. Many recently fledged (and renewed) feminist activists found their voices as they found their feet at the millions-strong marches that turned out in capital cities around the world. That energy continues to funnel into support for key causes and political representation for women. #MeToo halted or raised questions over the careers of some powerful white men and caused reverberations throughout thousands of workplaces. We can appreciate this energy and these successes even as we question the movement's limitations – such as the fact that the #MeToo movement was founded on a phrase created by a black female civil rights activist from the Bronx, Tarana Burke, but media coverage focused on the experiences of famous white women. Or the fact that the media has rarely been curious or diligent in exploring and reporting the experiences of poor women of colour at the intersection of sexism and racism. Or even that #MeToo never became #WeToo, an understanding that it takes a movement of many, not just a series of individual stories, to knock down structural inequality.

The recent outpouring of women's anger is too fresh to yet see its full impact, but the butterfly effect on conversations and attitudes is real. It continues to raise awareness of cultural and societal horrors, which allows us as female activists to start to chip away at some of the darkest and most deeply entrenched misogyny.

Shiori Itō was born in Kawasaki, Japan. In 2015 she was working as a television journalist in Tokyo, considering freelance options and with internships at several international media outlets lined up. Keen to find steady paid work at a respected news outlet, she wrote letters of enquiry to senior editors including Noriyuki Yamaguchi, Washington bureau chief at Tokyo Broadcasting Service, who replied to say there was indeed a producer job opening up. He invited her to discuss it in person as he was soon going to be in Tokyo.

To discuss that meeting with Yamaguchi and everything that happened after, Shiori Itō and I meet at London's Southbank Centre. It's a few months after we first met on a panel about #MeToo, around the time when her documentary about attitudes to sexual violence, *Japan's Secret Shame*, was shown on the BBC. We find a quiet corner and watch tourists drift across the balconies beyond us. As we prepare to talk through her experiences, I am anxious to protect her from any pain or discomfort in the telling. 'You need only talk about what you want to talk about,' I say. She nods, firmly, and then tells me what happened when she met the journalist she believed had her professional interests at heart.

'I met him after work one day,' Itō says. 'But after a few drinks, I felt dizzy and I went to the bathroom, and that was the end of the memory I have that day. The next morning, I woke up in pain and realised he was on top of me. That was the beginning of everything.'

Shiori Itō has become the face of Japan's #MeToo movement. She is not a woman at the front of a thronged crowd taking over the streets. Nor is she a leader of a feminist collective that has toppled influential men from their posts of power. Rape laws are so antiquated in Japan that the Deputy Prime Minister and Finance Minister Tarō Asō could say publicly that there was no such crime as sexual harassment and be speaking the truth. This extraordinary 29-year-old survivor is the lonely eye of a storm that has revealed the scale of women's institutionalised inequality in her home country.

Itō talks through the assault she endured and details how both her rejection of her rapist and the telling of his attack are in and of themselves acts of exceptional insubordination.

'In Japanese language there is a certain way you have to talk, as a woman, about older men. When we had the business dinner together, I spoke to him in that polite way. When the assault happened, I didn't know how to tell him to stop. Because saying it in that polite Japanese way didn't stop him. There is a saying in Japanese that "no, no" means "I like it."

I recognised that I didn't have a way to say no. So I had to start screaming in English to stop. I was screaming at him to fucking stop.'

Itō managed to get away. She tells me how it took her a few days before she could go to the police, during which she tried to work through the shame and confusion she felt at finding herself in a hotel room being attacked by a man she had believed saw her as a professional and able journalist.

'I wondered if it was something he had planned all along and just saw me as an object. We have been told as women to be careful all the time. In Japan assault was an everyday experience – as high school students we were molested and grabbed on transport every day. People noticed and ignored it. No one ever helped us. It was always the norm.'

Arriving at the police station, Shiori Itō asked for a female police officer. 'They asked me why, so I had to explain what had happened. When I finally met her, I had to explain it all over again. But then she said she was from the traffic department and couldn't do anything. So then I had to talk to a male investigator because there were no women in the crime investigation unit. But then they referred me to another department, and another. In the end I had to talk to six or seven different officers.'

As part of the questioning, Itō was made to act out what had happened with dummies. After that the investigators then said that as a sex crime it would not be possible to investigate. 'It's behind a closed door … in what they call a "Black Box" … Even when CCTV footage was eventually found of my attacker dragging me to the hotel – I had no memory of it – the investigator urged me not to complain because my career in Japan would be over and my family's reputation would be ruined.'

The investigation moved forward haltingly. At one point an arrest warrant was issued, but then withdrawn. The prosecutor working on the case was moved away and the case was given to a smaller police unit elsewhere in the city. In the end it was dropped.

In 2016 Itō went to a photographic exhibition about sexual abuse and, looking at the subjects, felt a visceral connection – and disconnection. 'One of the subjects had taken her life. I looked at the picture of her and I knew I was feeling the same thing she had been feeling. I was so ready to do the same. But then I thought, while I was alive I should use my life to try to do this work, while she couldn't speak up. From then on I decided to try every path.'

'The only way I could ask for the case to be reopened was to go to the Prosecutor Panel Committee – it's like a jury panel of randomly selected citizens. I had to gather my own evidence and witnesses. The case was dropped again, after a year. The conviction rate in Japan is 99.9 per cent. Prosecutors only prosecute when they know they can convict. The feeling was that people thought I was lying. So then I went public.'

In May 2017 Itō held a press conference to talk about her case. People warned her afterwards not to take public transport or to walk alone in the street.

'I thought they were kidding. But afterwards I started to see black vans in front of my house. I decided to move to a safe house. I stayed there for two months and didn't go out, but I did do more interviews. I wanted to be clear about what

I was trying to do. During that time, I got letters from women who had never shared what had happened to them. They said it was very similar. They were sure there was a date rape drug involved. I also received letters and emails from women saying how shameful it was of me to say these things. I wrote back to some of them, asking for a conversation so that we could start to understand one another better. But I never got any reply. My sense is that they had to live in that way because they couldn't do anything about it.'

'I hate what the perpetrator did to me. But my anger is for the system. All those investigators telling me to forget about what happened to me. It wasn't their fault. It was the system. They were not able to investigate because the crime wasn't written into law. They were protecting their jobs. The prosecutors were protecting their conviction rates. Everyone was protecting their reputations. Mine was the one that was sacrificed.'

'I didn't realise what kind of society I was living in. In Japan we can't say #MeToo. Our laws value objects more than women.'

In December 2019 Shiori Itō was awarded 3.3 million yen in damages against Yamagushi, who had repeatedly denied her allegations. The Tokyo district court that ordered him to pay her also dismissed his 130 million yen countersuit and ruled that she was 'forced to have sex'. 'We won!' she texted that day.

The anger of this extraordinary woman made it possible to start a conversation in Japanese media about sexual violence, even when the country's law, education system and very vocabulary made it almost impossible to do so. Almost as remarkable was Shiori Itō's ability to keep going and to connect with those who did not want to hear, with an anger that transformed and expressed itself into grief and forgiveness for many of those acting within an unforgiveable system.

This is what philosopher Martha Nussbaum, who believes that anger is overwhelmingly harmful, calls Transition Anger: when an individual chooses to focus on making things better for others rather than focusing on revenge or personal hurt.

Nussbaum does not make light of the challenge this involves. In her essay 'Beyond Anger', she writes: 'Anger greets most of us every day – in our personal relationships, in the workplace, on the highway, on airline trips – and, often, in our political lives as well. It is both poisonous and popular. Even when people acknowledge its destructive tendencies, they still so often cling to it, seeing it as a strong emotion, connected to self-respect and manliness (or, for women, to the vindication of equality).'

Nussbaum subscribes to Aristotle's view that anger inherently contains a desire for payback, something she cautions against as a senseless demand without a truly beneficial purpose. (Which calls to mind the quote by Irish-American actor and Green Party politician Malachy McCourt: 'Resentment is like taking poison and waiting for the other person to die.')

In the *Rhetoric*, Aristotle defines anger as an impulse, accompanied by pain, to a conspicuous revenge for a conspicuous slight that has been directed either at the person themselves or their friends. He says: 'Anybody can become angry – that is easy, but to be angry with the right person and to the right degree and at the right time and for the right purpose, and in the right way – that is not within everybody's power and is not easy.'

The 'right kind of anger', Nussbaum suggests, is the kind that can be transferred into revolutionary justice. It's the kind of anger that enables us to connect with multiple and intersecting inequalities, that enables us to understand and express solidarity with the wrong done to others – and thus be inspired to act.

Or, as Athena Stevens puts it, this is 'righteous anger, a force we need to change the world'.

'My activism is very much tied up with my faith,' Stevens goes on. 'I was raised in a Christian household and nearly every day growing up I was presented with the idea that we live in a very fallen and fucked-up world. My parents and teachers also made it clear I was very privileged in my life, more so compared to a lot of people with disabilities, so I'd better do something with these privileges. I say this because I think young women, specifically those from a conservative and faith-filled background, are often told that they should be meek and let go of their anger. But God gets angry. Christ gets angry. Buddha gets angry. What makes them angry is systematic injustice and the mistreatment of others.'

'Anyone who says people who are peaceful can't get angry, doesn't know their theology. As much as Christ said, "turn the other cheek", he never once said that about an issue around injustice. We are supposed to be angered by abuse, injustice, the squandering of human potential, those who devalue others, systematic discrimination and a refusal of responsibility. Any reaction less than anger is complicity within a hurtful system.'

I love Athena Stevens' call to arms. People of all faiths and none can feel righteous anger. I think, with time and practice and an understanding of ourselves, it's possible to interpret and reframe our anger into the power that Soraya Chemaly describes in her book: 'It begets transformation, manifesting our passion and keeping us invested in the world. It is a rational and emotional response to trespass, violation and moral disorder. It bridges the divide between what "is" and what "ought" to be, between a difficult past and an improved possibility.'

This is the best kind of anger management I've ever heard. Not an instruction to rein it in and rethink it, but to pay attention to it and where it can take you.

Laura Krarup Frandsen is still very angry. But, crucially, she's aware of the importance of her anger and the point of it.

'If we're not angry what are we fighting for? If I wasn't angry, would I be willing to get arrested, to spend all my energy doing this? But I think it's really important to use that anger as fuel and act from the anger, not in anger. If I want a better world and a more peaceful world, I have to act in peace. I think it's really important when we're asking for complete system change that we have to be part of the solution. We don't have to have all the answers – that's not our job – but we have to think about different ways of living, and if we're proposing a peaceful world in which we live with other values to what we see right now, we have to be part of that.'

When we listen to our anger, it becomes something else. Back to Nussbaum: 'In a sane and not excessively anxious and status-focused person, anger's idea of retribution or payback is a brief dream or cloud, soon dispelled by saner thoughts of personal and social welfare. So, anger quickly puts itself out of business. It looks more like compassionate hope.'

The idea that you can find compassionate hope from great hurt may feel like a stretch if you're only in the early phase of recognising anger and pain. But there is immense inspiration and encouragement in this promise. So don't feel self-indulgent about recognising your anger, voicing it and exploring it. Don't be afraid of connecting with your anger. Doing so is a step forward that can provide enormous learning and take you to a much more positive place – as we'll see in the next chapter.

3 WIELD HOPE AS POWER

'Hope is not a lottery ticket you can sit on the sofa and clutch, feeling lucky. It is an axe you break down doors with in an emergency.'
– Rebecca Solnit

Hope has such a bad image. It's soft. Something sweet and tender that's a poor resource in a gritty, bitter world. It's up against so much that is bad. How can it possibly be meaningful or useful?

I remember thinking this as a little girl of eight when reading my least favourite story in my favourite book. The book came from a second-hand shop and was old when I first read it. Judging by the style of the cover and the illustrations, I think it was probably published some time in the 1920s or 30s. It's got a cloth-backed hard cover that has become soft and threadbare, and the pages look like they were the kind that you had to cut open originally. And it has plates of painted colour illustrations. When I was little it was the most beautiful thing I'd ever seen.

It's a book of Greek tales and legends, rewritten for children. My mum, who was a classics teacher, gave it to me. She taught in an area of acute deprivation, to children from some of Glasgow's hardest streets. Those kids loved her classes because Mum told them the most bloodthirsty myths of wars and monsters and then asked the class to write their own alternative endings to the tales in which they could be the hero. (My personal favourite was one in which Hercules joined the circus and travelled the world as a lion-tamer.)

I loved those Greek myths too, though I wasn't so keen on the gods – it seemed as though they were always changing themselves into some kind of animal in order to harass mortal women. Creeps. I loved the goddesses, particularly Athena, the goddess of wisdom, and Artemis, the huntress, with her bow and arrow. They were so steely and noble and fearless. And they definitely didn't get bullied at school.

Among all of these rich and colourful stories was my least favourite. It was about a really boring woman called Pandora.

In my book, Pandora was sent off to marry Epimetheus, the brother of Prometheus who stole fire from the gods and thus infuriated them. Pandora's wedding gift was a mysterious box that she wasn't allowed to open. But she really wanted to open it, to such an extent that, as the book puts it, her husband had to 'scold her for her curiosity' – for what, after all, is more irritating than a woman who won't do as she's told?

Pandora resisted until she couldn't resist any more, and she opened the box. At this point, the story says, out of the box flew hundreds of stinging creatures. It describes them as: 'the dreadful and nasty things that are so disagreeable in the world today; things like measles and whooping cough and unkind stories and sums that won't come right and dangerously thin ice, and worse.'

What's left in the box after all the nasties have been let out is hope. And the story ends with the marvellously dismissive line: 'So you see, although Pandora did let loose everything that is disagreeable in life, she set Hope free, as well.'

As a child, I thought that was totally rubbish. Whooping cough in exchange for hope! Pandora was no heroine of mine. But as I read it again years later to my daughters, I realised how interesting Pandora is among these legends. The first human woman, sculpted out of the earth by the gods and sent to live with men, her name means 'the all-giving', for she was bestowed with gifts of charm and grace, and arrived bearing a casket of evil aimed at blowing apart a society of men who had sinned by coveting what belonged to the gods.

Pandora was the ultimate trick: so beautiful that men were dazzled and so disobedient that she could be relied upon to set loose what she had been warned not to touch. As the Greek poet Hesiod put it, Pandora founded 'the deadly race and tribe who live amongst mortal men to their great trouble'.

She is woman: the great, seductive spoiler of fun.

I had no idea as a little girl of the significance of this story. Of the significance of a heroine who brought hope into a world of angry men. But now that I am older and trying to be wiser, and have worked among female activists and with some of the most vulnerable people in the UK, here's what I think. I think the great trouble that women cause is not pestilence and sickness and bad sums. (Although I do spend a lot of my time pointing out the very bad sums of men in charge of spending taxes who seem to think that the only way to balance the books is to take money away from women.)

No. I think the most troublesome thing about women is the hope we bring into the world.

As a class of people who are oppressed by really bad things that didn't come out of a box delivered by the gods but which have been written into law and economics by men, the most daring thing we can do is refuse to give in to despair. Instead we dare to hope – an activity that doesn't come with a time-table or a measuring spoon. How long you have to hope for and how much hope you need is never fixed. We don't know for how many generations we must hope for change before change comes.

Hope requires discipline and endurance. It requires you to get out of bed every morning and reset your determination to make things better, no matter what setbacks you face. Hope is an action. And to act is to change the world.

'Hope means living. The day I stop hoping is the day I die! It is the force that keeps me going even when I can't see the benefits. It's the belief that tomorrow and the future will be better than today.'

These are the words of Joy Onyesoh, who works to build peace in Nigerian communities and in particular to support Nigerian women to be peace builders. She has led peaceful demonstrations to protest deadly attacks by armed Fulani herdsmen in Enugu State in the southeast part of Nigeria, and advocates for women's meaningful participation in peace pro-cesses, telling the UN Secretary General in 2018 that sustaining peace requires 'consistent and committed political will to challenge dominant narratives on gender, conflict analysis and power'. She has also run workshops for and with men's organisations to challenge the normalising of violent masculinity in conflict situations and, by exposing those assumptions, making space for women's voices and women's rights and thus paving the way to peace.

For Onyesoh, hope is vital for the tough work she does. When she talks about hope, it's clear that this is something with a real tangible presence in her work: 'Sometimes, looking at the level of work women activists have done and the changes on the ground, I feel so downcast. At times when I get a particular case of violence or discrimination, I am really moved to tears. One particular example is looking at Nigeria's recently concluded elections [in February 2019] and the way we had massive retrogression in women's representation. Just listening to women recount their ordeals is heart-wrenching, but at the same time it makes me more determined not to give up hope.'

As Onyesoh puts it, hope is a deliberate choice and one that inspires and gives strength to others to carry on too.

'Even if it's one woman at a time, the ripple effect is massive. This thinking now affects the way I design programmes. I pay particular attention to impact and stories of change. I strongly believe and know that ordinary women can change the world. I am an ordinary woman having a positive impact on my world, and I know that there are lots of ordinary women doing the same. It takes ordinary women to create this level of awareness that we are experiencing globally. That's the audacity of hope. I can't just stop hoping or believing in a better future.'

Another person particularly experienced at deploying hope as an activist tool is Ailbhe Smyth, a 72-year-old Irish academic and feminist activist who has worked for decades on campaigns to legalise divorce and same-sex marriage in Ireland, and most recently to 'Repeal the Eighth', the historic vote in 2018 which overturned Ireland's constitutional ban on abortion.

'There are levers of power, and they can be changed,' Ailbhe says. 'You have to think about history and know that the whole world is a history of change. And that in itself is the hope.'

Talking to Smyth about decades of activism, her clarity and resolve seem somehow innate. When I ask her how she became an activist, she replies: 'My mother always said that I was born busy. I climbed out of the womb early and caused her – as she once told me memorably in a birthday card – to have to "cancel many engagements".' Yet as Smyth talks it becomes clear this has been a lifetime's journey for her, and hope was something she did not always experience but rather learned along the route.

'I wasn't political when I was young,' she tells me. 'I was very focused on achieving the goals that my family had set out for me, which made me rather ill in the end. I got very severe anorexia and clinical depression, trying to be this high achieving young woman in a society that was giving me incredibly contradictory messages.' She explains: 'I had to go and get a degree and get a career and also toe every line: not be sexual, but get married and have lots of children – and still not be sexual. I got married at 24 and it lasted six months. I felt ill when I got married.'

Smyth spent the next five years in and out of psychiatric hospital. 'There was a huge conflict in me about who I was, what was I for, what was I doing with my life. Where was the evidence of any meaning to all this, and why was it such a hard battle all the time to make all of these disparate things fit? The only way out at the time was for me to fall ill and drop out of everything. That gave me time in which I was able to work certain things out for myself.'

In the following years, Smyth became increasingly politically conscious and started reading. During our conversation, she namechecks Germaine Greer, Andrea Dworkin, Adrienne Rich and Sheila Rowbotham – noting that their books had to be smuggled into Ireland. Smyth became an academic and realised that she was teaching exclusively male works to lecture halls full of women; she was unable to get a divorce; and she had become a mother to a daughter from a new relationship that the state decreed 'illegitimate'. So she began fighting the system that so limited her choices as a woman.

Smyth was named one of *Time* magazine's 100 Most Influential People of the Year in 2019. But the successful abortion rights campaign that catapulted her to more public awareness resulted from years of work on reproductive rights that began in the late 1970s with a campaign for access to simple contraception and moved through multiple different campaigns. As the challenges shifted and reformed, and the women's movement passed through different stages, Smyth started to understand the momentum of hope.

'The women's movement was very visible in the 70s, but in the 80s we had a very sharp economic downturn and there was a desire from some quarters to say: the women have said what they want. So there was a push-back. You come to appreciate over a lifetime that you're constantly in this coming and going, even though at the time you can feel that all has been lost. But you have to have determination to say: we simply cannot accept this fate, or the fate of another group. Activists are affected emotionally by injustice and inequality and the distress of other people. There are times when you will simply weep. But that's why you do it. Don't disregard the importance of emotion in motivating us to do what we do. That's what also gives you the hope.'

The Repeal the Eighth campaign first started, Smyth says, shortly after the government held a referendum in 1983 to insert, as she puts it, 'this horror' into the constitution. Abortion was already illegal in Ireland, but anti-abortion activists who worried that this could be changed had successfully lobbied the government for a public vote to add an amendment to the constitution giving equal rights to the unborn as to the pregnant woman. It read: 'The state acknowledges the right to life of the unborn and, with due regard to the equal right to life of the mother, guarantees in its laws to respect, and as far as practicable, by its laws to defend and vindicate that right.' The referendum passed with 66.9 per cent voting Yes and 33.1 per cent voting No.

'I was there at the beginning and end of the campaign. I cut my teeth on it. I then realised we needed to do a lot of our own thinking and started developing women's studies in Ireland. But I never gave up on that. Abortion was the great unresolved issue.'

In order to create a thinking space for feminists and activists that could sustain the abortion rights campaign, Smyth started the Women's Study Forum, where women could discuss issues affecting them and listen to women writers and artists. In 1990 she started the department of Women's Studies at University College Dublin, becoming a founding director of the Women's Education, Resource and Research Centre.

But campaigners for the right to abortion faced a long tough slog in the 1990s and 2000s, and some devastating cases.

In 1992, 'Case X', a fourteen-year-old girl became pregnant after she was raped by a man known to her and her family. She and her parents reported the rape to the Gardai and informed them of their decision to travel to England to have an abortion. Ireland's Attorney General obtained an interim injunction to uphold the 1983 constitutional amendment. Miss X returned home without having had the abortion. The High Court heard that she wanted to throw herself down a flight of stairs or under a train to 'solve matters'. Despite this, the court ruled that she could not travel for an abortion because the right to life of the unborn child should not be interfered with. Chased by the media and forced to move from her family home, Miss X was extremely distressed. By the time a Supreme Court appeal ruled that abortion was permitted where the mother's life was at risk, she was more than three months' pregnant. The girl and her family travelled to England after the injunction was lifted, but she then miscarried.

Despite the ruling that allowed for the threat of suicide as grounds for abortion, no government enacted legislation to enforce it.

In 2012, Savita Halappanavar, a 31-year-old Indian dentist, died in a Galway hospital from blood poisoning after doctors refused to grant an abortion. Halappanavar arrived at the hospital with back pain and suffered from an incomplete miscarriage. Despite asking repeatedly for an abortion, she was denied one, with one midwife explaining: 'This is a Catholic country.' There was still legal uncertainty regarding the precise circumstances in which the exception to preserve the life of the mother would apply.

Multiple referendums were held, yet progress moved at a snail's pace. The European Court of Human Rights ruled that Ireland was in breach of the European Convention on Human Rights. In 2013 the Protection of Life During Pregnancy Act was passed into law, making abortion legal in cases of emergency: a risk of loss of life from suicide or physical illness.

At that point, Ailbhe, who had been an active campaigner throughout, formed the Coalition to Repeal the Eighth Amendment, together with Sinéad Kennedy, a spokesperson for Action for Choice and another longstanding activist for reproduction rights.

Smyth explains: 'The country had changed. Thirty years is a long time. We had had an economic uplift, followed by austerity; after clerical child sexual abuse scandals and the exposure of the brutality done to young women and their babies by the Catholic Church laundries, generations of young people did not think the Catholic Church had any kind of authority over them whatsoever; social media had freed Ireland from the sense of being an island trapped in the past. It was my view that we had to stand up and take responsibility and stop seeing ourselves as poor, Catholic, hard done by. We were just another country, another democracy, that could do a hell of a lot better.'

The Coalition grew fast to incorporate not just abortion rights campaigners and the National Women's Council, but student unions, trade unions, doctors' campaign groups and political parties. When the Equal Marriage Referendum passed, Smyth was ready to catch that optimism and use it.

'I had had leaflets made at the local printers that said: "You Know What's Next" and I ran around the [vote] count centre and as people hugged me in celebration I would give them the leaflet. People felt that this was definitely the new Ireland now.'

In May 2018, Ireland finally voted overwhelmingly to overturn the abortion ban by 66.4 per cent to 33.6 per cent. The Eighth Amendment was formally repealed in September that year, with the Irish government recommending that women be able to access a termination within the first twelve weeks of their pregnancy.

Ailbhe Smyth is the personification of determined hope; the years of her determined campaigning, and that of thousands of women like her, against all odds, in the face of pain and privation and struggle, are an inspiration to every activist who has ever felt their hope flagging.

'You must never give up. Because change can come from such surprising quarters. Never lose heart,' Smyth tells me as we part company.

What's staggering is how for decades Irish society – and so many others – accepted such effrontery, such a basic inequality. Ireland's abortion history is just one example of how the state, religion and ruling classes can use ideology rather than violence to maintain power. They set policies to reinforce cultural norms that support their power – such as a ban on contraception or abortion, which reinforces the traditional male–female family unit, which keeps more women at home and out of work or politics where they could challenge men's power. Cultural propagation and enforcement of policy entrenches these norms as the status quo, making them extremely hard to challenge.

This goes on all the time around the world – think of patrician newspaper commentators dismissing the schoolchildren on climate strikes as irresponsible; or white social media influencers attempting to deflect the Black Lives Matter movement by insisting that All Lives Matter; or old white men leading the world's biggest companies who reject all-women shortlists, hire in their own image and say they 'just want the right person for the job'.

There's another name for bending people to the ideology of those in power by normalising their ideology. It's called cultural hegemony, a theory that was created by Antonio Francesco Gramsci, an Italian philosopher and communist politician who was imprisoned by Benito Mussolini's Fascist regime.

Gramsci also identified the creative challenge for every activist seeking to challenge cultural hegemony: the fact that hard reality creates an immensely difficult environment in which to be hopeful – yet hope is often the only thing that can bring about positive change in those circumstances. From prison, Gramsci wrote: 'I'm a pessimist because of intelligence, but an optimist because of will.'

Rebecca Solnit, in her book *Hope in the Dark*, goes one step further: the hope that societies attempt to deny us, intangible though it may often seem, carries more power than all the state media broadcasts and religious edicts can, because, she says: 'Belief can be more effective than violence. Violence is the power of the state; imagination and nonviolence, the power of civil society.'

Movements are marked by powerful and opposing surges in belief – the belief of activists in change and the belief of those who maintain that the status quo must hold. Ailbhe Smyth worked through these backlashes for decades. So did Gloria Steinem, who I met in London in 2016 when she came to talk about her first book in twenty years, *My Life on the Road*.

I talked to Steinem in the Emmanuel Centre, a hundred-year-old building with high-vaulted ceilings, tucked behind Westminster Abbey, where commentators, politicians and agitators often come together in public debates. On arrival at the event, I had to squeeze past swarms of photographers and hundreds of ticket holders queuing for their seats to watch this feminist icon be interviewed by actor and UN Ambassador Emma Watson – both women who hold superstar status for many activists. As I crossed the marble lobby and was guided by security staff towards a set of winding stairs that led to a small anteroom where Steinem was holding a series of pre-event meetings, I felt extremely anxious. I had been leader of the Women's Equality Party for eight months. I was at that time also running to be Mayor of London on a manifesto for equal pay, affordable childcare and an end to violence against women and girls in the UK capital. Our movement of political outsiders was growing fast. On the outside I was projecting huge confidence and reassurance and hope. On the inside I was frequently daunted by the growing public scrutiny of me personally and by the responsibility I held for the hopes and dreams of the women who were joining the Women's Equality Party with a strong feeling of having been let down by every other political party. I wanted to ask Steinem how she had maintained her composure and resolve over so many years; how she had coped with the furious aggression that men turn on public feminists; where she saw the chinks of light and hope for our movement.

I failed entirely. In fact, when I think back to that meeting, I can't actually remember the details because my embarrassment at what occurred has mercifully drawn a veil. I was so anxious to make the right impression and to collect all the answers I needed in order to support all of the women looking to me (as I felt it then), that I did little other than fluster. Steinem was patient and generous in later agreeing to discuss over email some of the things I had failed to explore with her in person.

I include this detail to show that you are never too old to make an idiot of yourself in front of your heroes. And also to demonstrate that, sometimes, when hope is all you have, it can feel overwhelming. When I had the opportunity to meet someone who had so famously carved progress with hope – something that, to me at the time, still felt like a flimsy and unpredictable tool – I was desperate to know what the trick was. Eventually, I realised that there was no simple trick, no single most important action. Over a lifetime in activism, Steinem had aspired to enormous change but distilled it into a series of daily actions.

When I asked her what she considered was the biggest challenge for feminist activists, Steinem replied: 'To behave as if everything we do matters – because it might.'

'We've lived with gender, racial and economic hierarchies for so long that it may be seriously hard to believe it's possible to live a different way – to be linked, not ranked.'

There is no silver bullet, nor a magic spell, nor a single miraculous thing that will unlock progress. We have to grow, administer and aspire to hope in all of our actions, all of the time.

I asked Steinem if she had expected, when she first became a political activist, to see women's equality in her lifetime. She replied: 'No, I wasn't that crazy. I wasn't fully realising yet that much of the country and the world was running on and profiteering from women's unpaid or underpaid labour. But I did realise that, if it had taken more than a century to win a legal identity as human beings for black men and for women of all races in the abolitionist and suffragist movements, it would take at least a century to win a legal and social equality.'

When I asked her when she first felt things shift significantly for the better, Steinem talked about the first National Women's Conference in Houston in the summer of 1977.

'The conference was the culmination of two years of organising, of electing delegates and voting on issues in every state and territory in two-day meetings that themselves were attended by thousands. Every step of the way, we were protested by right-wing religious, economic and racist groups. None of us was sure we could pull this off – but we did! Those 2,000 elected delegates made up the only economically and racially representative national body I've ever seen in this country, from Native Americans to newly arrived immigrants. It was kind of a Constitutional Convention for the female half of the country.'

After the conference, Steinem says: 'I knew the women's movement was huge and crucial; it was also as diverse as the country, but united even on issues like reproductive freedom and sexuality that had once been called divisive.'

The Houston conference was supposed to be life-changing for women across the United States. It created a manifesto – a National Plan of Action – for women, dealing with 26 areas across childcare, employment, equal representation, reproductive freedom and diversity. It was supposed to be heard and acted upon by government as a roar for rights. It was supposed to change history. Instead, Steinem now calls the conference 'the most important event that nobody knows about', adding: 'There was a backlash because we really were changing majority views. I began to fear that we would be treated as invisible or unimportant, no matter what we did.'

Houston provided a flashpoint for anti-feminists, anti-abortionists, evangelicals and the right. In organising a loud voice for progress, feminists inspired their opponents to organise, which they did so effectively that twelve years of Republican rule followed. Two years after the Houston conference, televangelist Jerry Falwell founded the Moral Majority political action committee, considered by many to be the birthplace of the Christian right that has since only grown its influence. Ronald Reagan secured power in 1980 and put in place a programme of 'Reaganomics' that included a reduction of the government spending relied upon most by poor women. He also opposed the ratification of the Equal Rights Amendment and signed into place the policy known as the Global Gag Rule. This policy, which withholds funds from any non-government organisations (NGOs) that provide or advise about abortion care, was upheld by President George H.W. Bush who succeeded Reagan, and was imposed again by George W. Bush and Donald Trump. The International Center for Research on Women has said that this policy has reduced access to voluntary family planning for women around the world as NGOs have been forced to curtail or end their work, which has in turn resulted in increased rates of unintended pregnancy and pregnancy-related injuries and deaths, including from unsafe abortions.

Houston stands as an emblem of hope, and also of just how much hope is needed when the backlash comes. Ireland stands for hope, and what can be achieved when it is channelled against the backlash. Today, women campaigning for abortion rights are warriors skilled in using hope against hypocrisy and cruelty all around the world. The interactive online world map provided by the Center for Reproductive Rights is a multicoloured chart of misogyny, detailing the scale of women's inequality from countries where abortion is banned outright, such as Nicaragua, Gabon, Egypt; to those where abortion requires permissions that render it virtually impossible, such as Poland, Saudi Arabia, Thailand; to those where reproductive rights are being rolled back, such as the United States, where President Trump is relying on federal bills that lie about the existence of a foetal heartbeat at six weeks of pregnancy, even as doctors protest.

Women's bodies and abortion law are pivotal in thinking about hope because it's the first battle for freedom that we face and thus our first test of determined optimism. As Gloria Steinem reminded me, the battle for reproductive rights is about 'first causes: females have the one thing that the patriarchy doesn't have – wombs – which is why controlling reproduction by controlling women's bodies is the first step in every unearned hierarchy. Diminishing violence against females and restoring our control of our own bodies is the most crucial step for all women. Whether we can decide when or whether to give birth is the biggest determinant of whether we're healthy or not, educated or not, active outside the home or not, and how long we live.'

Ilyse Hogue is the president of NARAL Pro-Choice America, the oldest and one of the largest abortion rights advocacy groups in the United States. She leads and oversees the organisation's efforts to achieve reproductive freedom for women, via advocacy and political action, reaching from grass-roots organising and canvassing to lobbying, and endorsements of and donations to pro-choice politicians. When I ask her how she manages to work with hope in one of the worst environments for women's rights in the United States for decades, her answer surprises me.

'I'm an ecologist by trade, and as an undergraduate I studied geology,' Hogue begins. 'I try to take comfort from understanding how brief a time period this is, though that doesn't lessen my understanding of the pain being inflicted on people and extracting a huge toll. As an ecologist, I understand how resilient the system is and that we will survive – I don't mean me or even humanity, but this essence of what is life and what is good will survive.'

I say, 'Yes – but what about Trump?'

Down the phone line from Washington DC, Hogue laughs and says: 'The proverbial strongman is actually weak because what they fight for is not popular. From a US-centric view, what we're experiencing is that Trump and the party that supports him is having to resort to increasingly undemocratic methods to push through their policies because they don't have support – either by voter oppression or packing the Supreme Court.'

'They are holding on by a thinner and thinner thread and, while it is terrifying to see the lengths they will go to, to hold on, I really have a deep belief in the power of people to recognise the collective good and act in service of it.'

Like Ailbhe Smyth and Gloria Steinem, Ilyse Hogue is also very clear that the fight for abortion rights lies at the heart of many bigger battles. That thought sustains and drives her.

'I do really believe fighting against reproductive oppression is the heart of fighting for collective power,' she says. 'Reproductive oppression is grounded in misogyny and racism and control by a small group of individuals over a larger group of people. It's the nucleus of intersection of greater movements about how we throw off the yoke of control and gain collective freedom.'

Our bodies. Our rights. Our equality. Our hope. All are interlinked.

Or, as Rebecca Solnit puts it: 'It is striking that the people with the most at stake are often the most hopeful.'

My copy of Solnit's *Hope in the Dark* has been so many places with me, sitting in my bag like a talisman through some of the hardest experiences of my campaigning life. The idea that hope could sustain and nourish and inspire struck me like a thunderbolt; it changed me entirely as an activist and even now regularly helps me to move again when despair and anger threaten to stall me. I love everything about hope. When I say it, I see the colour yellow. I hear wind in the trees and believe the planet can survive. I remember my mum singing Joni Mitchell songs as she headed off to meetings of the Women's Liberation Movement, of which she was a member when I was a child. I think about my own youngest daughter's grin early every morning as she manages to intercept me for a cuddle in bed. I feel my friends' arms in mine as we sang and marched down London's central streets with a million other women marching for their rights.

But I also think of it in the days and nights when I am sad, and reason feels broken and progress so far away, and idiots clog up television and radio with regressive ideas and a carelessness for the future that feels like a personal insult to my children. On those days I turn to hope as well, because Solnit helped me to understand that hope is the ultimate act of defiance. It is something that you can learn and apply yourself to; it is something you can grow until, far from seeming eccentric, it appears in fact to be the only sensible and appropriate course of action. Even in the moments when it feels like your side is losing the generations-long battle for progress.

Solnit concludes: 'How do we get back to the struggle over the future? I think you have to hope, and hope in this sense is not a prize or a gift but something you earn through study, through resisting the ease of despair, and through digging tunnels, cutting windows, opening doors, or finding the people who do those things.'

Kris Hallenga is a perfect example of one of Solnit's people – those who are digging tunnels, cutting windows, opening doors. Her Instagram account – a series of colourful, active and often very funny snapshots of her campaign under the handle @howtoglitteraturd – prepares me well to meet this ray of light in person.

We meet for lunch at a healthy fast food chain in a train station, for Hallenga is making time for me amid a busy schedule of meetings to talk about her ten-year campaign to educate women to feel confident and knowledgeable about their breasts.

'I was 22 when I found a lump in my breast, and the first GP said it was hormonal and nothing to worry about. That was exactly what I wanted to hear because I was about to go off and travel and leave England behind, and I didn't want her to say, "Stay here and we'll do some tests."'

'Then I noticed the lump was getting more painful. When I came home seven months later, I went back to my doctor's surgery and saw a different person who said, "It's still fine. I'm not worried about this. You're a young person." But my mum wasn't convinced. So, I went back again, and my normal doctor reluctantly referred me because I asked for it. I had an ultrasound, and they said to go away for three weeks to see if things settled down. In those three weeks I'd wake up with a blood-stained t-shirt. When I went back, I took it as proof. Then they did a mammogram and a biopsy, and that's when they told me it was breast cancer.'

It had never crossed Hallenga's mind that she could have cancer. She thought it didn't happen to young people, an attitude mirrored by healthcare professionals in all of her initial appointments. She knew of no one in her peer group who had had it. She had no other link to it.

'I was frustrated. I was pissed off. But I thought: I don't want to be angry. I need to concentrate on getting better. I didn't realise at this point that I probably wouldn't get better. They did further tests, and a week after my initial diagnosis I was told it had spread to my bones. I thought: Well, this is not ideal.'

This seems like an extraordinary response. But Hallenga shrugs, spears some more broccoli, and says: 'I'd never considered what I would do if I got shit information like that. It had never crossed my mind. So, when it did happen, I thought: What is the point of wallowing right now? I have to just get on with treatment. I was quite frightened. I didn't know what was going to happen. But the breast surgeon never said, "Your prognosis is …", and I'm so glad he didn't. I emailed him on my ten-year anniversary the other week and thanked him for never putting a time limit on my life. Because I've seen that happen to many people, and they live by that. It becomes their expiry date. I am so glad that he never did that to me.'

Hallenga began radiotherapy, followed by chemotherapy. She started a blog, initially 'just to get the words out', and increasingly began to feel an urgent need for a campaign – one that was focused on giving young women the information that they needed to know their bodies intimately and well.

'I felt, this needs to be bigger. This education needs to be mainstream. That's when I got some family and friends around my mum's dining table. We weren't talking about charity at that point. For young people, the attitude to charity so often is, "Well, I'll give money to this, but there's never going to be a solution for it." So, I thought I wanted it to be more of a campaign, more activist – get the word out there, get it done, and then pack up and go home.'

She began by writing to the organisers of a student festival and asking for permission to attend.

'We didn't even think about fundraising. We didn't take buckets or anything. My sister and I were face-painting near the main stage, and when someone asked how much it would cost them, we said: "Make a donation." Then they would sit with us for five minutes, and we started a conversation about boobs, about checking yourself, and getting checked out if you noticed anything. No one left crying or distraught or frightened. It was simply a conversation about knowing your body. It was clear that it was about cancer, because I was there with no hair, doing this thing – but I was having a jolly, a nice time – and so it was clear that cancer needn't be as shit as you think. It was great on so many levels.'

Hallenga founded the CoppaFeel! charity with a specific focus on helping young women know how to examine and spot any changes in their breasts, but with a wider educational remit via the #RETHINKCANCER campaign to encourage all young people to learn about cancers and healthy lives from a young age.

'I want [young women] to take action because it's down to them to check their boobs and know their bodies and take responsibility for their own health. So we stand a better chance of surviving breast cancer when we stop relying on other people to educate us about our own bodies. We should know our bodies better than anyone. We should be working as a team with healthcare professionals.'

'I've had to be way more proactive in order to survive this long. If I wasn't like this, I don't think I'd still be here. I know my body really well. I show it more kindness. Rather than hating the cancer – because the rhetoric is that it's an evil thing and we should hate it – I respect it. It's a very clever disease. I don't want to hate a part of my body. So I work with it, figuring out what it is trying to do and what I can do about that,' Hallenga says.

Kris Hallenga has won awards for her inspiring activism; she regularly writes cheery, accessible columns for the UK's most popular tabloid newspaper; and she's delighted to see that the government is adding cancer and checking bodies into the personal and social health education curriculum for secondary schools in the UK. Fundraisers for CoppaFeel! run marathons wearing one jolly giant inflatable breast. Teams of university students sign up for awareness-raising campaigns that involve hanging self-check guides in the bathrooms of university halls of residence. Hallenga's social media feed advertises a 'booberella', with a video clip of her laughing and ducking behind a breast-shaped umbrella while someone off-camera directs a fire hose at her. She has choice words for traditional campaigning approaches to cancer.

'I was in a TV advert for cancer; I was cast as the illest because I had no hair, and I was asked to say the kicker line: "because it isn't a fight we always win". I shared that line with someone else, who died. I felt really sad and also cross. The people making the advert didn't consider that might have had a huge impact on me at all. So much of cancer campaigning is about death and sadness rather than living with it, which is a very different place. I'm sick of the victim stuff. It's so done.'

'When I see our university boob teams come to our events and hear them say it's the best thing they've done, to know they can make a difference, in such a fun and engaging way, it blows my mind. I wish I had been like that when I was younger. Everyone else's issues were their issues. Not mine. It took cancer for me to say: "Oh, I can have a positive impact."'

Again and again, it seems to be that women's activism is marked by this gritty, no-shit optimism. Whether it's expressed deliberately or incidentally, hope for change and hope in activism marks women's rebellions and challenges in a specific way.

Gudrun Schyman, founding leader of Sweden's Feminist Initiative sees it too. 'Women have always had a positive attitude to change,' she says. 'It shows up in so many places when you look closely – in campaigns on the climate, for peace, for migration. The traditional role of being a woman is to see also to other people's needs outside of your own. But we also know as women that challenging the power of patriarchy takes time and [therefore] that we have to do what we can do during our own time on the planet.'

A key part of that, she adds, is 'incorporating this idea of sharing and caring outside of gendered roles'.

Schyman first attracted public attention in her home country in 2004. After national crime figures for 2003 showed that a woman was murdered every week, that there were five attempted murders every week, and six rapes every day,

Schyman suggested a government investigation into the cost to society of male violence against women. She also proposed that men should settle the account. While the media jumped on her 'man tax' idea, Schyman set about organising a political feminist response. Feminist Initiative – also known as Fi – started as a pressure group and quickly evolved into a political party, garnering support from US actor-turned-activist Jane Fonda and Benny Andersson, founding member of the pop group ABBA.

Schyman grew the party one conversation at a time, in a painstaking process of travelling personally around the country meeting and persuading. As she reminisces, I realise not for the first time – for Gudrun and I have worked together for a while now – how similar her experience feels to the months I spent criss-crossing the UK between 2015 and 2019 to canvass potential members and supporters for Britain's feminist party, the Women's Equality Party.

'As a volunteer organisation, Fi had no money or resources to arrange meetings around the country, so we had to ask people to gather at least a group of 25,' Schyman says. 'I had meetings from morning 'til night, six days a week. Sometimes the groups were quite samey – all students, or a big group of friends. Sometimes they included up to three generations of voters. One particular meeting had only men. It was extremely interesting to see how they reacted when the question of men's violence against women was discussed. By the end of that meeting, only one man maintained that he had never sexually harassed anyone.'

It took Fi nine years of contesting every national and EU election to win its first seat, in 2014, when Soraya Post was elected to a seat in the European Parliament. In the same year, Fi won seats in thirteen municipalities, including in Gothenburg and Stockholm.

Hope carried them through the years of slog, Schyman says. 'What if the suffragettes had quit after ten years, saying protests were not useful or significant? Where would other countries have got their inspiration?'

She adds that, for her, hope is about a particular perspective – and one that she didn't at first realise she had. 'I have very small rear-view mirrors! I concentrate on what's in front. I look to the future. The very first time Fi ran for office, in 2006, we got 0.9 per cent of the vote. I still declared us winners because we had done something that no one else had done before us: we had declared feminism as an independent ideology in parliamentary work. That was bigger than the result that we ended up with.'

Solnit writes about the challenge to hope that is posed by the people with very big rear-view mirrors: cynics who hide their despair behind black humour and 'yes, but'; fantasists who hark back to an imagined glorious past when they didn't have to share; the perpetual whatabouterers who duck any responsibility to act because there's always that bigger challenge to point to. Those people are the ones who scoffed at Gudrun's 0.9 per cent of the vote. They're the ones who scoff at the young people protesting the climate crisis. They're the ones who have poo-pooed New Zealand Prime Minister Jacinda Ardern's budget of big dreams – a world first 'wellbeing' budget that directs billions into services for mental health, child poverty and family violence. If you've started to flex your activist muscle or even just cleared your throat on social media, you've met some (some days it feels like you're meeting all) of these folks. They're not all trolls. They're scared and they've been living life too long trying to be invisible while others take the blows. They have forgotten that hope is possible, but 'they' can sometimes become 'we', as Solnit observes: 'It was as though many of us didn't know how to be this other kind of person, this person who could speak of big dreams, of high ideas, of deep emotions, as though something small-scale and sarcastic was the reduced version of self that remained to us.'

In 2018, after the first three years of the Women's Equality Party had included an EU referendum, a snap general election, multiple local elections and a mayoral election, against a backdrop of growing hate crimes, division and political confusion, I made a promise to myself to be an optimistic feminist. I chose those words deliberately, because I could see that I was living through a time that required hope almost more than anything else. In these times, hope is our greatest support. Hope is our strongest armour. You can't conquer a person who has hope. When everything around you seeks to make you despairing, angry and lonely, hope is the ultimate act of joyful revolt.

4 COLLABORATE WITH COMPASSION

'I learned compassion from being discriminated against. Everything bad that's ever happened to me has taught me compassion.'
– Ellen DeGeneres

My daughters and I are watching daredevil caterpillars.

It's a Sunday evening and we are curled up together on the sofa watching David Attenborough's *Our Planet* on Netflix. The natural world's best-known and most effective advocate is demonstrating two essentials of activism: storytelling and how collaboration is vital to survival.

Against a backdrop of waving grasses, Attenborough introduces a species of butterfly, the Alcon blue, which resides in 'the ancient hay meadows of Hungary, still farmed in the traditional way'. In his sonorous voice, Attenborough explains that each female must mate and lay eggs on just one species of plant – the Marsh Gentian – that soon hatch into caterpillars.

'High up on the plants, they're safe from predators below,' he tells us gravely, as the scene cuts to lines of translucent amber ants with fearsome mandibles patrolling grains of sand. The music takes on a mildly threatening air as Attenborough intones: 'But then the caterpillars do something seemingly suicidal. They abseil down on threads of silk to the ground below and into danger.'

My girls and I are open-mouthed. Betty shrieks and pokes me as one black-faced, purple-speckled fuzzy caterpillar lands, bunches and squirms along the ground for mere seconds before it is seized upon by an ant and hauled away.

Attenborough explains to us that the caterpillars have no defence at all against the ants, but they are producing a scent like that emitted by an ant's larva in order to incite precisely this scenario. On screen, a caterpillar is borne, legs waving feebly, down a dark hole in the ground, across the rattling clatter of rushing ants. The ants are taking the caterpillars back to their nest, where they deposit them in the colony's brood chamber, among the ants' own white larvae, where, despite being a shockingly different colour and shape, the caterpillars give off just the right signals and the nurse ants rush to feed them.

'But there is more. The caterpillars now start to mimic the sounds made by the queen ant and, as a result, the ants treat them like royalty,' Attenborough tells us. Seventeen-year-old Grace makes a sound of appreciation. 'They give them such quantities of food that the caterpillars grow hugely. And there, underground, the caterpillars feed and grow for nearly two years. Until one day there is nothing for the ants to feed. The caterpillars have pupated.'

From our sofa we burst into applause as, in a tiny tunnel, from a yellow walnut-shaped cocoon, crawls a crumpled cornflower-blue butterfly. On trembling legs, it walks slowly up towards the entrance of the burrow before taking flight and joining the others that dip and glide above the grasslands. 'This complex life may be labour-saving for the butterfly. But it's risky,' concludes Attenborough. 'If anything happened to the ants or the Gentian, the Alcon blue would become extinct. Only tiny fragments of these ancient meadows are left in Europe.'

In other words, the survival of the butterfly depends on the survival of the ants and the Marsh Gentian flowers, which in turn depend on the survival of the ancient meadows. So much for survival of the fittest. This is survival according to complicated teamwork: a leap of faith from a place of safety in order to find the right allies and persuade them to work with and for another species altogether, while counting that other forces will similarly work together to maintain the surrounding fragile botanical ecosystem.

It's not just the Alcon Blue that needs to do this. We all do.

In his book *Team Human*, Douglas Rushkoff writes that: 'Nature is a collaborative act. Evolution is every bit as much about cooperation as competition. Survival of the fittest is a convenient way to justify the cut-throat ethos of a competitive marketplace, political landscape and culture. By viewing evolution through a strictly competitive lens, we miss the bigger story of our own social development and have trouble understanding humanity as one big interconnected team.'

I've seen so many great ideas wither and fade because their owner either could not or would not share them. Collaboration is at the core of successful activist campaigns. Offering up your idea to be considered by others makes it stronger and more beautiful through multiple reflections and refractions. This comes easily to some campaigners; others learn the difference it makes through experience. Similarly, some causes attract attention and sympathy more easily, which is swiftly followed by offers of collaboration. Others are harder to get momentum behind, often because they challenge a taboo or force the public to confront their own bias and prejudice, lack of knowledge or complicity in everyday unfairness. And, of course, those are the campaigns in which collaboration and cooperation is even more important.

All of this came as essential campaign experience to Amika George, who was seventeen when she started her Free Periods campaign.

'I was having breakfast before school, and I saw a report on my phone that a charity based in Leeds, which provided free menstrual products to schoolgirls in Kenya who couldn't afford them, had been contacted by a couple of schools in Leeds, saying they had the same problem. The schools had noticed a pattern in their absence records of girls being unable to come to school because they couldn't afford pads and tampons. So the charity, called Freedom4Girls, had to redirect that product and start doing the same thing that they were doing in Kenya in Leeds. That really shocked me,' she says.

George started to read more about the subject and discovered several reports across the UK about British girls having to use alternatives like tissue paper, newspaper, socks, t-shirts – whatever they could find in place of sanitary towels and tampons. Her shock was compounded when the government remained silent on the matter.

'I expected something to happen straight away. That the government would say they would give them to those who needed them, or provide them for free. And that didn't come. And that for me felt really wrong, especially when I talked to people about period poverty. I'd previously never heard of it, no one else had heard of it, and no one I knew had suffered through it. It was a big revelation, a silent problem that no one was talking about. That seemed really wrong.'

George started a petition on Change.org, called #FreePeriods, with the demand that girls on free school meals, from the lowest socioeconomic background, should be eligible for free menstrual products too, provided by the government.

'Growing up online and being a teenager, I'd always associated activism with the internet and always thought that if you want to spread a message and get an idea out there, why wouldn't you use the internet when you have a tool that enables you to speak to and connect with so many people? I worked really hard to get as many signatures as possible – I sent it to all my friends and family, my parents' friends; I got my brother to send it around his boys' school, which he was reluctant to do. I had to pester my dad too, but in the end he sent it around his work.'

'The more I thought about it, the more I realised that not enough people were talking about it because of the stigma around menstruation. No one wants to talk about periods; and then when there's something around poverty too, it was really easy for the whole issue to be completely hidden. And the more I thought about that, the more I realised this was a feminist issue. The reason we don't talk about periods is misogyny, because we live in a fundamentally patriarchal society where periods are thought of as gross and disgusting and exclusively a women's issue. So anyone who doesn't get a period feels they don't have to get involved.'

By this time, George tells me, she was working hard for her A-levels, and also emailing everyone she could think of to support her #FreePeriods campaign. 'If I turned on the TV and saw a presenter, I would find out their email and write to them. If I noticed someone on Twitter with a particularly large number of followers, I would contact them to ask them to share it for more signatures.'

By this time, there had been a snap general election, during which Amika George persuaded the Liberal Democrats, Greens and Women's Equality Party to commit to the #FreePeriods pledge in their election manifestos. The Change.org petition bore hundreds of thousands of signatures from the public, and many celebrities had come on board. But still the government had not acted. So Amika decided to organise a street protest, working with the Pink Protest, a community of feminist activists supporting each other to make change by exchanging tips and advice.

'I met the co-founders of the Pink Protest, Scarlett Curtis and Grace Campbell, and we talked about what we could do together. We decided to organise a protest for 20 December, the day that all the state schools in the UK broke up for Christmas. It was a lot of work. I'd never organised a protest before and had no idea how much work goes into it, like contacting the council, telling the police, getting speakers, getting a stage and microphones and stuff – and then actually getting people to come!'

The team communicated via Instagram to their target audience and 2,000 young people turned up. The resulting crowd was a joyful party. 'Even though it was protesting against such an awful thing, it felt like a celebration. There was a real sense of solidarity among everyone – it was like 2,000 friends getting together, waving banners and singing. It felt like the best day of my life.'

Three months later, the UK donated £1.5 million from its tampon tax fund – collected from VAT on menstrual products – towards addressing period poverty. In April 2019, the UK government pledged funding for free menstrual products to be provided in all English schools and colleges, a scheme that was rolled out in early 2020. Free Periods is working with teachers and student activists to ensure schools opt in to the scheme. They also launched a social media campaign, #FreePeriodStories, encouraging people to post their stories to help end the shame and stigma around menstruation.

While the work is ongoing, she has formed some early conclusions: 'One of the biggest things I found was how much value there is in collaboration and just working with people who are equally passionate as you on different things. At the beginning of the campaign, I did feel as though I was doing it all myself, and it was hard because there was so much to do – and it was only me. But there's so much value in using different people's skills and resources and time and dedication. When you collaborate with people who are like-minded, amazing things can happen.'

George's impact and experience are interesting in many ways, not least because they demonstrate a fine balance between social media collaboration and face-to-face street protest. Again and again while campaigning, as a mother raising money via running challenges, or as an ambassador of UK charities such as National Autistic Society, or as leader of the Women's Equality Party, I used social media to find and organise within networks of like-minded people. But I frequently found that space as challenging as it was sustaining. Humans have reached increasingly towards technology to shore up our fragile ecosystems of support and communication, but I fear this is now becoming reflexive behaviour – an assumption that tech is always better.

When we seek to organise, tech often separates us. The social networks that encourage sharing the details of our lives too often discourage collaboration, encouraging us to set up personal profiles and distil ourselves into ever more concentrated versions of our fundamentals until we become products. Our likes and dislikes have become commoditised by the entrepreneurs and businesses of tech, determined to compress us into fixed individuals whose data they can sell on to corporations. This process turns our outward-looking instincts to connect against us, as we join these networks only to find that we are encouraged to define ourselves by our differences.

Furthermore, the platforms upon which we joust didn't anticipate this type or level of conflict and have done very little to protect users against the pain it causes. The trolling, the pile-ons and the abuse were never factored into the lines of code that built the arenas, because they were built by predominantly young, straight, white men who don't personally encounter the misogynist, racist, ableist vitriol that their platforms routinely host. So there are no systems to anticipate and prevent harassment.

As Douglas Rushkoff points out, the internet, like television before it, was supposed to be a connector. But as populists and corporates got hold of it, the internet too, became a place to insert fantasies, from politics to products, that push individualism, self-branding and desocialisation, the cost of which we are only now starting to understand as our social media addiction propels us to compete against each other for followers and 'influencer' status. The stress and pain this can bring is real. Our nervous systems are still working as though these interactions are life or death. 'Threats to our relationships are processed by the same part of the brain that processes physical pain. Social losses, such as divorce or expulsion from a social group, are experienced as acutely as a broken leg,' Rushkoff says.

All of this means that, unless we are aware, careful and strategic about how we use tech, it can make collaboration more difficult rather than easier.

'When media is programmed to atomise us and the messaging is engineered to provoke our most competitive, reptilian sensibilities, it's much harder to muster a collective defence. We lose our ability to distinguish the real from the unreal, the actual from the imagined, the threat from the conspiracy,' Rushkoff says.

In short, it can really affect our capacity to listen. Our empathy, our capacity to understand and identify with the

thinking and motivations of other people – is being diminished. The oppression of the poor and the 'different' as part of
power struggles among the wealthy and influential have marked
human behaviour for millennia. Now social media risks further
entrenching many of those prejudices, as it reduces us to ava-
tars in divided, distant communities.

In 2014, British feminist writer Reni Eddo-Lodge wrote a blog
post declaring that she had reached the end of her capacity
to discuss racism with people who refused to accept the limits of their understanding of it. Under the title 'Why I'm No
Longer Talking to White People about Race', she wrote of her
exhaustion with the diplomatic niceties of attempting to engage
with defensive prejudice: 'Amid every conversation about
Nice White People feeling silenced by conversations about race,
there is a sort of ironic and glaring lack of understanding or
empathy for those of us who have been visibly marked out as
different for our entire lives, and live the consequences.'

The post went viral and Eddo-Lodge went on to write a
bestselling, award-winning book on the subject. When we meet,
she's just emerging from a long period of touring with the book
and talking about race. It's five years since the blog post, and
I'm curious whether she sees a different level of engagement
now from white people than when she wrote the article.

'I was thinking that I was done with the feminist movement. It was a general fatigue of trying to have a conversation
in a movement of white women who appeared to be committed
to stopping that conversation from happening,' she replies. 'Am

I being heard now by white women? I think the particular white women I talk about in the book – largely no. More broadly, yes. But it's a shame that my work, packaged in a legitimate mainstream presentation, was what it took to have many white women sit up and take notice of anti-racism. Because it's not dissimilar to what black feminists have been saying for a very long time.'

If racism is to be defeated, white people must do more to understand how they benefit from systemic privilege. Further, they need to do this work without asking black people to explain it to them, or look for reward and approval as part of the process. As Eddo-Lodge puts it, she's not 'looking for school reports'.

Collaborating means meeting with open minds and compassionate hearts. It means being comfortable with feeling uncomfortable. It means doing the work to discover the extent of what you don't know. It *doesn't* mean using those with different or extensive experience as a crutch, or expecting them to be a personal mentor or a conduit for your own frustration. Be inspired – but then start your questions or conversations with 'we', rather than 'you'.

'When I travel with the book, overwhelmingly I receive the same frustration as I was articulating in that blog post, so actually it's really difficult for me to be on the receiving end of all that. The book was to help people think critically about the world around them. I end up saying to my audiences: please talk to each other, rather than telling me how much the book means. I would much rather they meet more like-minded people and make connections between one another,' says Eddo-Lodge.

The emphasis here is on meeting in the real world, she adds. 'I don't think social media is an effective tool for having conversations with people. They're better done in private. On social media there's a whole bunch of people watching. These platforms that say they're going to connect us more meaningfully actually just expose us and have really no accountability. They don't allow for complexity. They don't allow for nuance. Face-to-face meetings are the most affirming activist spaces that I've been in. Activism is in community.'

So maybe when we think about collaborating, we should start by working out what the best space is for that work, and how we might use available tools to make initial contacts. We could consider using social media tactically – just as a first step to make first connections that we take offline into fresh collaborative spaces. We can rethink our screwed-up social connections by using technology judiciously. We can work to bridge the divides forged by populists and entrepreneurs, by insisting on our own physical community spaces again, and in building those afresh, we can recognise the impact that the lack of them has had on how we relate to and rediscover one another. And in turn what that says about the priorities of those with power.

Despite being inherently social, humans have long had to battle the imposition of man-made systems that separate us from each other. Before social media turned us antisocial, dominant Western economic ideologies did the job. The template that economics set for human behaviour is long out of date and doing a lot of damage. Maybe by unpicking that we might start to reframe the rest.

In the summer of 2019, I receive an invitation from a consultancy that helps public services collaborate on social challenges. It's a panel discussion with audience participation to consider how we can build a collaborative society. I'm delighted – and fascinated that it's being held in Canary Wharf. During my twenty-year career as a journalist, I reported on business, markets, trade and macroeconomics, from London's financial centre, the Paris Bourse and Washington's Department of Commerce. The prevailing themes, as I recall, were greed and fear. Solidarity? Not so much. But I go along to this meeting with great interest and find myself sitting in a room at the top of a glittering tower, with views out to a cluster of encircling towers. Below us is a gargantuan shopping mall, a restaurant complex for meals and deal-making at any hour, and multiple bars where men in suits, weary of managing Mammon, loosen their ties over a drink at the end of each day.

At the front of the room is Kate Raworth, an economist known for her writing on 'doughnut economics' – a model that balances essential human needs against Earth's ecological ceiling. She speaks vigorously about framing a successful outcome as 'thriving' not 'growing' and summarises neatly how previous economists mistakenly arrived at the conclusion that man's self-interest was the only driving force, and the only thing that could matter. I listen and smile and remember tearing through Katrine Marçal's book *Who Cooked Adam Smith's Dinner*, stunned to think of the intellectual limits that could produce a theory of individual self-interest while failing to see or comprehend its dependence on the social support provided by a mother who made his meals and cleaned the study around him. According to Raworth, however, nineteenth-century political economist J.S. Mill is the real baddie of the story for ditching Smith's secondary theory that interest in others is how we make society work. Thus was focused all future Western theory on 'rational economic man, characterised by self-interest, knowing the price of everything', as she puts it.

'We need to tell ourselves a different story of who we are if we are to stand any chance of thriving, all 10 billion of us on this planet,' Raworth says. 'Economics classes start with "here is the market", but we all wake up in the household – the love economy on which so much human wellbeing depends.'

Raworth lays out the interconnected arenas in which we live and work – areas which our economic models should take into account, instead of narrowly focusing on capitalist supply and demand. There's the household; the state – in which we can be a citizen, a public servant, a voter and/or a protestor; and the commons – a self-selecting community that creates the goods and services we value, in which we can be a co-creator, a sharer, a repairer, a collaborator. At the end of her presentation, Raworth urges us to shake off the reductionist view that we're only ever shopping or working, and curate our own local 'Makerspaces'.

My heart jumps in recognition at the description of the commons, which sounds so much like the community support spaces I have personally been lifted by and in turn have tried to create myself. The 'Makerspaces', collaborative workspaces, ring with recognition too as I think of the feminist learning that I've gleaned from such places. I'm intrigued to find more examples, and spend the tube journey home glued to my phone, researching other models of this new collaboration.

My search leads me to Todmorden, a town of about 15,000 people in West Yorkshire. It sits in the heart of three valleys created by the Pennine hills that run through the North of England, separating west from east and putting a boundary around Yorkshire. The hills are very scenic. The town itself, which boomed with cotton mills and canals during the Industrial Revolution, has struggled at times during recent economic downturns to maintain the beauty of its civic buildings and spaces as well as its community pride. But visit it today and among the first things to strike you is how much grows in the town – literally. From wooden planters full of herbs at the railway station to orchards in the grounds of the doctor's surgery to beds of salad leaves outside the college of further education, Todmorden is bursting with life. Community activist Pam Warhurst explains:

'I come from a red-brick middle terrace. I was the first of my family to go to university. So, I could see how some people experience life, but I also know how my home community worked: the lack of opportunity, the problems caused by the divisive education system, the issues around the dominance of the male agenda at the expense of the female agenda. That whole lack of investment in joy.'

Warhurst used to be the leader of Calderdale Council, the local government authority for Todmorden and many more towns and villages across the Southern Pennines, and was also a senior member of the Countryside Agency, tasked with improving England's rural affairs. For years she watched leaders above her meet to discuss the state of the environment and then fail to act; in between she also observed the detachment of those dependent on the council services she worked to provide. Struck by the stasis on either side of her, she had a moment of breakthrough – one of those glorious activist lightning bolts that sometimes strike and show us the way forward.

'I lived through the disappointment of the Rio Earth summit, and the summits in Copenhagen and Kyoto, where leaders of nations came together and said, "We need to change," and then went back to business as usual. I went to meetings in London where people warned the end was nigh. And at the end of one of them – I remember, it was 2008 – I thought: I've waited and waited. Why don't we just see what we can do ourselves? It was a moment of clarity beyond belief that it was down to us to do something.'

'I asked myself: What do we need to do to engage people who have never thought it was part of their lifestyle to be able to do anything about this? It seemed to be that food was the obvious part of that conversation. We didn't need conversations about peak oil. We needed actions that engaged the people who lived on my terrace.'

'Food is the shared language of opportunity. We eat together, we grow together – we have to do it, and you don't need a degree to do it. Food brings together sustainability and self-belief.'

Pam Warhurst wanted to create something that would awaken in local people a sense that they could be active participants in their community – and also demonstrate to confounded policymakers what could be done with a bit of imagination. On the three-hour train journey back from her

London meeting, she sketched out plans on the back of a napkin and shared them with friends on arriving home.

'In all the high-level meetings at Kyoto and the rest of it, the voice that was missing was of the ordinary person who cared about their family's future. So we created a model that would plant food and create jobs and enterprise from it. If our children grow up passing our own food in our own villages day in and day out, it seemed to me that they would have a different approach to their environment and themselves. You'd have an ability to wake up in the morning and do something and then to collectively demonstrate that you care about your community and you have a voice and a view on what happens to it,' she says.

So began Incredible Edible. From a public meeting in a café, organised by word of mouth, a group of local residents decided to grow local food and local jobs. Three in particular came forward who would become the organisers: Mary Clear, an excellent community networker; Estelle Brown, who at just shy of 70 years old trained herself to design a website and build a social media presence; and the suitably named Nick Green, of whom Warhurst says: 'Our Nick just wants to plant everywhere. Give him two seconds and he's got raised beds.' They didn't ask permission and they didn't ask for money. They scavenged for seeds and wooden boards and they began to plant.

'The first place was a grass verge on the side of one of the main roads into Tod,' she recalls. 'When we got there, it was a dog toilet. We put on our rubber gloves and we cleared it up, took out the empty tin cans, and we planted food. Within a few months, the council had started to mow the grass – without being asked – and put a park bench in. And now there are cherries growing there, and herbs, and people stroll by and sit down. It was propaganda gardening. We created an initial space where people could meet and talk about food,' she says.

Emboldened, the team sought out more and more public space in which to plant. Derelict public buildings, such as the old medical centre, became green spaces where fruit, herbs and vegetables sprouted. The activists painted green the hoardings that had been erected to cover up buildings in disrepair, and created avenues of apple trees and beds of rhubarb around them, putting up seasonal signs to advise locals when the fruit would be ready for picking. Around the new medical centre, they took out inedible prickly plants placed for show and instead created an apothecary garden. Then they headed for the police station.

'It was flat and concrete, and we planted sweetcorn – a genius idea. Because sweetcorn's not native to Tod, but it does grow taller than the police!' Warhurst explains with a shout of laughter.

No one vandalised the food-growing areas. Community relations improved. Local traders selling their own local food put up signs so that people could see where to find more local produce, and could shop there as well as picking herbs at the train station and filling bags of salad from the local college grounds. In turn, more people set up stalls at Tod's local market to sell more local food; and local cafés in turn cooked and sold more local eggs, bread and beer. Pam Warhurst and her team are now having conversations with the police and health and rail companies about how to keep momentum going with more local policies.

'This is not about community gardening,' she stresses. 'It's about learning how to live differently with food and create jobs out of it.'

Ask her about collaboration and she raises her hands outwards, palms up – a gesture that simultaneously invites people in and says such an action is obvious.

'Decide your cause and then work out what your piece of the jigsaw is. You are never the full picture. You are only a piece. Look at what other pieces you need to come together. Then you start to see that you can create a picture of chance with other talents. You learn about learning from others and creating opportunities you never imagined.'

Melati and Isabel Wijsen are all about the jigsaw. These young women from Indonesia have built a global anti-plastic movement, Bye Bye Plastic Bags (BBPB), from a single decision they took to try to clean up their local beach.

To understand the scale of their ambition and their task, let's first consider this: according to Indonesian Environment and Forestry Minister Siti Nurbaya Bakar, some 6.8 billion plastic bags are used in Indonesia each year and almost 95 per cent of those plastic bags end up as waste. Indonesia is the world's second largest producer of plastic waste after China, according to research published in *Science* in 2015, and much of its archipelago – 17,000 islands – is in dire straits in terms of waste management. On Bali, where Melati and Isabel live, waste removal services could not keep up with the number of discarded plastic bags. Heavy rains would flush torrents of them into the sea.

And once-beautiful beaches became regularly swamped by tides of litter, bringing misery to marine and human life alike.

'It was 2013 and we were in middle school. We were ten and twelve years old at the time,' Melati Wijsen remembers. 'We had a lesson about world leaders who had made an impact in their communities – people like Nelson Mandela and Mahatma Gandhi. We didn't want to wait until we were older to start making a difference. We realised that we only had to ask ourselves the question: "What can we do as kids living on this island?"'

'BBPB started without a business plan. We had no strategy. We just had a vision to make our island home plastic bag free. We had no idea of the journey we had just started,' she adds.

Having decided to try to clean the beaches, the sisters gave a speech at a school conference in an attempt to reach more students and ask for help. 'Isabel and I were super nervous. There were about 50 students in the audience. We wrote our speech out word for word and had to bring the piece of paper with us on stage.'

More students joined them, and Melati and Isabel Wijsen drew more collaborators by organising events around the island. 'We would sit with the village elderly and with local communities and talk. We brought all the island together to find solutions towards a more sustainable future. We hosted a fun run to raise funds for our NGO, we had artists play songs; other collaborators gave workshops.'

The sisters' organisation and impact grew alongside their collaborative practices. They held Bali's largest ever beach clean-up, which attracted 12,000 volunteers. They gathered more than 100,000 signatures to petition the local government for action. They were increasingly invited to give talks at environmental conferences for action.

'One of our first successes was when we realised the impact we had on youth globally,' Melati Wijsen tells me. 'In 2016 we had our first reach-outs from young people around the world who wanted to implement BBPB in their home countries. This was so surprising for us! It was so empowering and motivated us even further.'

BBPB now operates in more than 30 countries around the world to clean up environments by educating people on the importance of removing plastic and offering practical ways to do so. Its website lists among its values innovation, collaboration and passion, and offers toolkits, videos and a helping hand to get started to anyone who clicks on the link to join the movement. At home, it has distributed educational booklets for primary school children across Indonesia and distributes alternative cloth bags to local shops. And Bali has now banned single-use plastics – including plastic bags.

Melati Wijsen's advice is simple. 'Surround yourself with people that can help take up your idea and take it to the next level.'

To be an effective activist, you need to be bigger than yourself. Your own story is just the starting point. As activists, we have to see and hear each other and create spaces to find our common ground, from which we can build networks to grow our own resources and raise our voices. We need other people to grow a movement because only movements can bring about change. So we have to be able to do this with, and care about, people with whom we may share little apart from our humanity – the strongest bond of all.

Minna Salami describes herself as a 'liberation strategist'. I know already from her journalism and from discussions that she is a brilliant activist, an awareness-raiser and an organiser, but when she lands on this new term we both laugh in recognition. It's the perfect term for her.

I first heard Salami speak as part of an organised event to discuss the #MeToo movement and was struck both by her succinct analysis of why the movement had not brought real structural change and by her clarity of vision for the kind of feminist movement that could truly bring a transformation.

'As women we're replicating old and dominant patterns in our activism. We want to be the first person who got women this, or who built that. We don't see collaboration straight away as crucial because we are socialised into this individualistic competitive society. But collaboration matters because we have the same or similar aim, which is to be free of oppression.'

She continues: 'If I want to build a house but I only have a hammer, while you have bricks and someone else has a spade, then in order to get the house we want we all have to build together. You have to work out the best way to start and how you can make a home for everyone who is participating in the building of it. We are all coming with different knowledge. We all know the ways in which the dominant forces are preventing us from building this home because of our different experiences. We all have knowledge. So our collaboration is crucial.'

Minna Salami's example demonstrates how compassion is the key to collaboration. It's the start of understanding the different layers of experience and perspective outside of your own. Without compassion you can't get to empathy. And empathy, which truly places you beyond yourself, is the only effective way to achieve change.

'Empathy is about caring for others but also caring about the movement. What is the point of being involved in the feminist movement if you're not listening to others? It's completely futile,' says Salami, who was born in Finland to a Nigerian father and a Finnish mother. 'I've had so many instances of racism from white women, from feeling that my Finnish grandmother never quite saw a cause of pride and beauty in me that she saw in my white Finnish cousins; or teachers who accused me of plagiarism when I wrote of very personal experiences, to editors who said my book was too African. But when I say I am a feminist, I am talking about sisterhood not just patriarchy. Regardless of my hurtful and traumatic experiences, I stand in 100 per cent solidarity with all women – black and brown and poor and white. I can't pinpoint the exact moment in which I realised how important that is. But I really and truly feel it is the only way that we are going to succeed with the aim of feminism.'

Minna's empathy and solidarity are inspiring – and the result of deliberate hard work based on an understanding of why both of those things matter. As she explains: 'I lead by example and I work on myself. Nobody is empathetic by default. I notice that when I express empathy, I inspire other women to do the same. If you go into a space with the attitude of "My experience is the worst and everyone should learn from me," then you are creating a huge wall in terms of the movement moving forward. Whereas if you go into a space with "I am here to learn and to teach with reciprocity," then you are able to affect the energy of that space. And others want to reward you back with the sentiment that you are affording them.'

Empathy is like a muscle. We have to work it regularly in order to make it stronger and more flexible. Understanding this, says philosopher Roman Krznaric, 'is about recognising two things. First, that the capacity to empathise is part of our genetic inheritance, with roots deep in our evolutionary pasts. And second, that empathy can be expanded throughout our lives.'

The next job, as Reni Eddo-Lodge and Minna Salami have pointed out, is to make an imaginative leap into the life of the person with whom you are attempting to empathise. Recognise the barriers put up by our culture and society and politics, and work your empathy muscle to dismantle them. In his book *Empathy*, Krznaric uses the powerful example of Oskar Schindler, who started World War Two as an acquisitive Nazi businessman indifferent to the fate of Jews, but who, on getting to know the people who worked with him, went to tremendous lengths to save them. 'Schindler's story tells us that the act of empathising begins with looking someone in the eye, giving them a name, and recognising their individuality. It is about acknowledging their humanity in defiance of prejudices and stereotypes; it is about refusing to obey authorities who command us to denigrate them.'

I've learned through a decade of activism that the only way to develop this close understanding is to work alongside people.

To join organisations, projects and clubs with people who are not like you, to have physical encounters and to practise conversation with people whose lives are very different to your own. If that thought fills you with dread, take comfort from the fact that many of us find it hard. If tolerance and understanding were easy, we'd be living in Utopia. If admitting the limits of your own knowledge were easy, there'd be a lot less war.

When I was first grappling with my daughter's autistic behaviour – about half-way through the years-long process of getting a diagnosis for her – I went on a training course for parents of children with special educational needs. I was exhausted from our constant fights and endless negotiations. Where I saw black, Grace would see white – and this was just over practical things like teeth-cleaning and getting dressed. Our daily life had become a series of aggressions as I tried to navigate her through school and home life and she clung to her need for deeply specific systems and structures. I couldn't understand for the life of me how my precious child and I would ever free ourselves from this combat. I had stopped listening to her, approaching every conversation as arbitration. When I arrived to start the training course, I was in similar mode: belligerent from tiredness and unoptimistic about outcomes. But by the end of the day, I felt entirely different: energised, clear-headed and ready to build a life with my lovely girl.

The course was run by UK charity Mencap, which works to build a society where people with learning disabilities are valued, supported and included. The premise of this particular session was to provide support to parents of children who could only say no to them. Many in the room were bringing up children who had a diagnosis of Pathological Demand Avoidance (PDA), often a characteristic of autism, which drives a person to avoid everyday demands and expectations to an extreme extent. It's behaviour that stems from huge anxiety that both comes from and creates a need to be in control. My daughter's problems with social interaction and communication were prompting her to restrict all other behaviour until she could get to a point where she felt she might get a grip on the topsy-turvy world around her. Over the course of that afternoon, I learned that while Gracie could only say 'no', I had effectively only been saying 'too bad'. I had to learn to work backwards from her 'no', along her train of thought and figure out what was prompting that refusal. I had to put myself in her shoes, rather than superimposing what I would do in that situation and assuming that if I said it enough times, she would do the same. I had to walk Grace's path to walk us both towards an agreement.

The lessons that I learned in that classroom have stayed with me my whole life. I am very far from being a star pupil, but I am grateful to my daughter every single day for all that she has taught me about embracing difference and the need for truly immersive empathy.

The other thing I realised back then was that wanting to advocate for a particular cause or community means you have to look at your own actions as a member of that community. It's not enough to simply point the finger at other people's faults. As a campaigner you must not consider yourself exempt from the hard parts of the conversation.

Nim Ralph is a community activist who is also a trainer, facilitator and strategist for other activists, providing workshops and programmes for UK campaigning organisations like Campaign Bootcamp and Movement Builders. Ralph first got involved in activism through the climate movement following the G8 meeting at Gleneagles, Scotland in 2005, and became aware of the need to address the dynamics of internal collaborative practices; they began to facilitate sessions for the Climate Camp gatherings, which acted as a foundation for direct action against major carbon emitters.

'I have an inclination towards establishing processes in groups. It balances getting shit done with working out the means towards the end, thinking about whose voices are heard and how you are doing it so it's not just the loudest people shouting over others,' they tell me. 'At Climate Camp we rotated the responsibility, but I felt particularly pulled towards it. Then I had an awakening that these places are wildly white and ableist and middle class. For a while I internalised that as meaning that there was something wrong with me. But then I realised I'm not white and straight and from the middle-class background, and that's why I have a different perspective on the ways we're doing this.'

'There is a sense in these spaces of "we're good people doing good work", and it's felt as if that's enough. It's the blight of the left, and it's where real progressiveness and real movement for change gets stultified. Because people's sense of self is bound up in the work that they are doing, it gets hard to disentangle behaviour from identity,' Ralph says. 'Regardless of whatever kind of politics or activism we're talking about

– capitalism and work, consumption and the environment, or white supremacy and race, or patriarchy and gender – we're lining ourselves on one side as "good" versus "bad", but we're not addressing the fact that we all also behave a certain way within those systems.'

From that point, Ralph set up and worked in a series of organisations aimed at providing training and building relationships between communities. A cornerstone of that work is to bring a wide variety of activists and campaigners into the same space: climate change campaigners alongside asylum seekers and anti-poverty campaigners and disability justice activists. 'The theory of change around that is that it supports the movements to develop relationships and provide much more cross-fertilised thinking; so they can consider what analysis they're not so far bringing to those campaigns,' they tell me.

Listening also provides an essential opportunity to slow down and regroup. 'I create spaces in which campaigners and activists are forced to take time to stop and reflect on strategy and how and why they are doing things in a focused and constructive way. Many of them are bound up in a sense of urgency and don't stop to reflect on behaviour, and what they're doing stops being strategic.' It's a particular issue in the climate movement, Ralph reflects. 'As long as I've been in it, we've had a sense of how many years we've got left – ten years, then eight years – and saving the planet becomes more important than an analysis of justice in how we save it. The climate is the only thing that really poses an existential threat to white middle-class people, and this is why they get this massive urgency around it, and it's hard to get them to do a race and class analysis too.'

Ralph is energetic, cheerful, thoughtful, aware of the joys as well as the dogged diplomacy required by this work, and tuned in to the great need to talk and be emotional about a subject that drives people into activism.

'Most campaigners are really driven by their heart. They think: "If people just knew what I knew, they would think the same and do the same as me." But you need your head and your hand as well as your heart. For effective campaigning and ways of reaching people, we need to engage people in thought and through understanding; through using our hands to take action and move things forward, and also through engaging people emotionally.'

I'm in a hotel room in Sarajevo, the capital of Bosnia and Herzegovina. I'm here to engage in a dialogue between women community activists working for peace. We are about 50 in total – a few from Geneva, some from London, but the majority either from the Balkans or Syria, working in the aftermath of war to rebuild. Their task is enormous: the day-to-day work of re-establishing some kind of normal among a traumatised and dispersed population, while also still tracking down the missing and forcibly disappeared; seeking justice, recompense and reconciliation; and also trying to influence and change structures – economic, political and societal – so that a fairer future can be built. They do this even while institutions like the International Monetary Fund and the World Bank negotiate with leaders who have, in many instances, been directly involved in the violence. The women here are on the ground doing tough work that requires many hours of practical effort as well as a bottom-less capacity for nurturing patience. As civil society organisers, community mediators and those seeking to be the next gener-ation of collaborative politicians, they are wearily familiar with the well-functioning, well-oiled industry of war and its routine aftermath. But they have a palpable energy for change. As one woman says during our discussions: 'They put people who had been holding guns yesterday into positions of leaders for peace. What nonsense. You build peace with people who have always been building peace.'

My role, my invitation to come, was to offer some thoughts on political organising. But once here, I feel overwhelmed and inept, faced with experiences and challenges for which I can (with confused gratitude) find no comparative basis. We sit, mostly women, apart from one or two men, at circular tables arranged around a ballroom-sized function room. There is no hierarchy, no panel discussions. We all wear headphones. Behind a glass screen along one wall, translators work to move Arabic into Bosnian into English, and back again, facilitating the exchange and flow of ideas and experiences and questions. I don't speak at all on Day One. On Day Two I give my name but little else. I am sleepless from the electrifying coffee they serve here, and also from being so very challenged to offer col-laboration that won't be just empty words.

On the evening of the second day, we all walk into town for dinner. We leave our mirrored tower block that was built with Saudi money to replace the burnt-out shell of the previ-ous hotel, obliterated during the war. Then we walk along the river, past communist-era tower blocks from the 1960s. They are riddled with bullet holes. Passing through alleys notorious for previous scenes of brutal sniper fire, we then proceed along streets lined with ruined pink and grey Austro-Hungarian baroque: once-pretty buildings with broken windows, boarded-up doors and graffiti, overgrown grass at the gates. Further along, the buildings flatten and change again to the low red roofs and bustling cobbled streets of the old Ottoman market.

I am walking along with a young woman who has helped to organise this event. As we walk, she points out areas of the city that have been marked for demolition and rebuilding, and expresses her concern that unscrupulous landowners are lining their pockets at the expense of Sarajevo's cultural history and collective memory. She is one of a group of activists who are organising to fight the sale of the land. Judging her to be in her late twenties, I ask her if she remembers anything of the war. Smiling softly at my question, she tells me about growing up in Mostar with a Catholic mother and a Muslim father, and about the war within a war that left her city even more devastated than the one through which we currently stroll. She tells me about their next-door neighbour, a Croat, who denounced her father, which led to her father being taken to a detention camp. She tells me about being caught by a bomb blast that left her unable to walk for four years. She tells me about travelling to Paris to study, then to Hungary, at a university which has now been closed down by the far-right populist government. I tell her I am sorry for my clumsy question and that I can't imagine what she has been through. She puts her arm around my waist. And she tells me that her mother returned to Mostar after the war, and that the same neighbour who denounced her father now looks after her mother. He is sorry, she tells me. When she visits her mother, she now says hello to him again.

The loving generosity of this woman floors me. Throughout this week, her co-activists working for peace have told stories of others' pain and loss, asking for advice on how best to help them, to advocate for them and to advance their cause. I realise now, of course, that these women all carry their own stories of suffering and endurance and also forgiveness. The amount of pain they carry and how much they have been able to put down in the spirit of love and in order to move forward with compassionate collaboration is extraordinary.

In the former Yugoslavia public space has been reduced to ethnic space. Bosnian, Serbian, Croat and Muslim children are educated separately, and their families live apart, relocated to areas in which their tribes gather in greatest numbers. In a land with such a rich history of ethnic pluralism, identity has been divided and reduced. It does not feel like a solid ground for peace. As the slow-moving justice process becomes ever more opaque; as the career reconstruction contractors of the international community repeat old patterns in a new colonialism, the women working for peace here must work even harder, against all the odds, to collaborate and find common cause. They are setting the bar for all of us.

5 PRACTISE PERSEVERANCE

'But still, like air, I'll rise.'
– Maya Angelou

Just as there has never been a more vital time for our activism, so the environment for activism has arguably never been tougher. As we've discussed, we are up against an aggressive political environment, a cynical and divided public, a widening gap between the very richest and the poorest, and technology and media firms that get rich from our gladiatorial combat. Working our way through this minefield, our anger, hope and compassionate collaboration will be vital for success. But so will our staying power.

In a nutshell, we need to learn how to keep going. Like many activists, I initially made the mistake of thinking this meant working on how I could recover quickly and decisively from difficulties – spring back to shape, if you like. I thought also, particularly during difficult campaigns and media interviews, that the skill lay in being able to endure unpleasantness.

If I could learn simply how to mute my distress, then I could succeed as an activist. To a certain degree this is true, but it also forces you to spend a lot of time thinking about yourself in a way that can be dangerous – you end up absorbing the punches and even sometimes feeling like it's your fault that you're feeling the pain of them. Alternatively, you work on getting a thicker skin, so you simply feel everything less. This approach also leads to failure: either you become less feeling, less compassionate and less able to work effectively; or else you expend precious emotional energy wondering why you are 'too sensitive'.

To be clear: you do have to look after yourself. Health advice – such as doing exercise, getting enough sleep, eating well – is all really important. I find that connecting with the natural world is also increasingly important for me as I do this work. There is an energy and also a calm in the majesty and scale of mountain ranges or seascapes that reassures me that whatever is bothering me will pass; that I am tiny and insignificant in the grand theme of things – and, thus, so is whatever's bothering me; that it is possible to just *be* for a while. But one of the aspects of the current popular discussion about resilience that really bothers me is its core implication that you personally are the thing that has to be worked on. As I suggested at the start of this book, 'resilience' has become a buzz word, often used to suggest that we must simply bear up better under the weight of injustice rather than protest it. A focus on resilience, for example, allows corporations and institutions to redirect the public to their own failings by recommending training or gym subscriptions or vegan lunch options on Mondays – rather than themselves addressing the sexist workplaces, unpaid care work, hunger and privation, and unfairness that are really bending us out of shape.

We need to talk about how we keep going, for sure. But we need to do that within a framework that keeps the focus on the problem that we are trying to solve. It's an 'eyes on the prize' approach, if you like, that will enable and encourage you to keep thinking of the various ways you can come at the issue and deal with the inevitable setbacks and failures and difficulties you will experience, without feeling that these are your personal failing. That's why *perseverance* is what counts, rather than resilience or endurance.

Think of Sisyphus, the Greek king who, according to mythology, was punished for his cruelty by having to roll a boulder up a hill and watch it roll back down, over and over again. Endurance is being strong enough to roll that boulder up the hill every day again and again. Resilience is rolling that boulder up the hill every day knowing that it's going to roll down from the top once you get there. Perseverance is working out how to get that boulder up to the top of the hill and get it to stay put.

I'm fully aware that I'm taking liberties here with Sisyphus – after all the myth is about illustrating futility and laboriousness. But we can rewrite the myths we've been told. And our starting point needs to be that in the hardest times, our efforts are needed more than ever.

So, when we're thinking about keeping going, we need to start by deciding who will help us do this and how to engage them in what we're doing. That means talking about what you're doing in the hope of engaging other people in the same work, to achieve effective campaigning and a stand a better chance at a good result. And, since we're talking about challenges in this chapter, the first you are likely to face is that of '*whataboutery*'. It's a classic for all campaigners.

Consider the following interactions:

ACTIVIST: Hello, I'd like to talk to you today about ending violence against women, which is rising sharply in the United Kingdom—

WHATABOUTERER: What are you doing about women's rights in Saudi Arabia? They have it much worse there. Why aren't you doing something about that instead?

ACTIVIST: Hello, I'd like to talk to you today about ending the climate crisis and some everyday actions that we can—

WHATABOUTERER: It's getting hotter on Mars and Pluto too. What are you doing about that?

ACTIVIST: Hello, I'm raising money to fund training for girls to learn code. There's a big gap in the number of women learning technology compared to men because—

WHATABOUTERER: What about the boys who haven't learned to code? Why don't you care about them? Are you just being massively sexist?

And so on.

My first piece of advice regarding whatabouterers is to determine as quickly as possible whether that defensiveness is something you can gently dismantle in order to have a proper conversation. My second piece of advice is that a simple 'and' to acknowledge their point can often deflect this: 'Yes, AND I care about that too, which is why …' My third piece of advice is that, in many cases, such people are not engaging in good faith but rather to deter you, slow you down and score points on a subject about which they don't actually care. If, by some amazing coincidence, you happen in your campaigning to come across someone who is actively campaigning for a cause that is an alternative to yours, then you can shake their hand and wish them well. But the fact is that those who protest that you should spend your time instead on Saudi Arabia, Mars or encouraging more boys to enjoy maths are generally not them-selves campaigning for those things in their spare time. For that reason, *you absolutely do not owe them your time.* You do not have to engage in battle with those who are simply battling for the hell of it. Conserve your energy for those who can be converted to your cause. The devil already has enough advocates.

As Theodore Roosevelt said: 'It is not the critic who counts; not the man who points out how the strong man stumbles, or where the doer of deeds could have done them better. The credit belongs to the man who is actually in the arena, whose face is marred by dust and sweat and blood; who strives val-iantly; who errs, who comes short again and again, because there is no effort without error and shortcoming; but who does actually strive to do the deeds; who knows great enthusiasms, the great devotions; who spends himself in a worthy cause; who at the best knows in the end the triumph of high achieve-ment, and who at the worst, if he fails, at least fails while daring greatly, so that his place shall never be with those cold and timid souls who neither know victory nor defeat.'

Or, as research professor and bestselling author Brené Brown alternatively puts it: 'If you are not in the arena also getting your ass kicked, I am not interested in your feedback.'

Poorna Bell is a mental health campaigner dedicated to talking more openly about suicide. She says her approach to talking about suicide is to be able to have that conversation in a neutral space that means that both sides are being listened to. 'The whataboutery and aggression starts because, when you start talking about activism, you're basically saying that there is a topic and you are at one end of it. So, if you are going into conversation with someone who may be at the opposite end of where you are, their guard goes up – rather than listening to what you have to say, they are already concocting reasons to dismantle your belief system.'

Bell was plunged into this field owing to the experiences of her husband Rob, who had chronic depression and addiction issues. She talks of 'firefighting', of dealing with the day to day of Rob's difficulties, until he died by suicide. At that point: 'There was stuff I knew, statistics I knew, about mental health, but I hadn't lived them yet. Then, when that stuff has destroyed your life, you are faced with certain choices: to do what a lot of people who are bereaved by suicide do, which is, because of the stigma, to never talk about it, or to make destigmatising it part of your life's work. I found the silence around it was just unacceptable.'

'I realised that the Office of National Statistics was not recording suicide by ethnicity and background. I know, because I come from the South Asian community, how bad they are about talking about anything mental health related and particularly suicide. It's a hugely emotional subject, but I managed to talk about it in a way where the emotion doesn't undermine the clarity of what you need to come across.'

'What I notice is that when you can frame things and explain them in a way that doesn't automatically dismiss another person's point of view or where they might be coming from, it is much easier to get people to listen … It's a very fine line in terms of framing what you want to say without assigning blame or scolding other people.'

Poorna Bell is very clear on how she makes space to have these conversations, and how she has learned to take herself out of that space in order to conserve her own mental health and energy with a view to being able to keep campaigning. In addition to learning how to deal with those who present false arguments or who react with anger, another key element of perseverance is finding ways to safeguard your mental and emotional reserves. Bell is strategic about how she uses her time, how much of herself she gives and how she assesses other people's contributions. Here's how she does it:

'A lot of the times, you're met with someone who is using your views to project how they see themselves. When someone has posted something really mean about something I've done, I'm thinking they're not being heard in their own life. Increasingly, I'm seeing a lot of women being really loudly shouted down. But a fundamental aspect of activism is understanding why things are the way they are and how you can change them. Sometimes it does involve people getting a bit uncomfortable. People need to listen a bit more.'

But how do we listen more? What does getting uncomfortable look like? One of the most challenging aspects of activism is how you keep going with your discussions about the stuff that really matters to you when you have a point of difference with other activists – the people who are indeed in the arena and who you probably quite like or respect, or are in all other ways ready to work with. Disagreements with this group is the part that's most likely to shake your conviction and most likely to really hurt.

First things first: consider what stage of discussions with your allies you are in. If you're in early collaboration, consider whether your discomfort comes because you're still stretching your own perspectives. Consider whether you need to sit a little longer with that discomfort before deciding that you disagree. Make space for further conversation. And if you're still really struggling, consider the option to agree to disagree, to let your thoughts continue to turn in your head. Give yourself time to mull things over and keep considering. In the meantime, look for common ground in other possible areas of collaboration instead.

All of this is hard. As Nim Ralph has pointed out, we often bring our personal experiences into our campaigning, and for that reason a criticism of our campaign or our idea can feel deeply personal and hurtful. And because activists are passionate, exacting and dogged, our arguments with each other can go on and on … and on.

In 2017, Frances Lee wrote an essay called 'Excommunicate Me from the Church of Social Justice'. Fed up with the impossible, dogmatic standards of activist culture, they wrote: 'There is an underlying current of fear in my activist communities and it is separate from the daily fear of police brutality, eviction, discrimination and street harassment. It is the fear of appearing impure.'

How many of us have hesitated to speak up or contribute our thoughts on a subject for fear of being found to be less than perfect? How many of us have chosen not to engage in a subject that we care about for fear that self-appointed arbiters and gatekeepers for that issue will find our thoughts too messy, too difficult or too problematic and hand down poor scores in front of a booing public? How many of us have wondered why such an insistence on purity of purpose and message doesn't leave room for grace and forgiveness? And how many of us feel frustrated at the resulting lack of nuance from all of the above?

Lee goes on in their essay: 'I am always ready to apologise for anything I do that a community member deems wrong, oppressive or inappropriate – no questions asked. The amount of energy I spend demonstrating purity in order to stay in the good graces of a fast-moving activist community is enormous.'

'Activists are some of the judgiest people I've ever met, myself included,' they continue. 'At times, I have found myself performing activism more than doing activism. I'm exhausted, and I'm not even doing the real work I am committed to do.'

Lee's essay is scorching. As a queer, trans person of colour (QTPOC), they go on to criticise the 'colonialist logics' of that community: 'I reject QTPOC supremacy, the idea that QTPOCs or any other marginalized groups deserve to dominate society. The experiences of oppression do not grant supremacy, in the same way that being a powerful colonizer does not. Justice will never look like supremacy.' The essay goes on to criticise an activist culture of preaching and punishment and the limitations of instructive articles that restrict further questioning.

Every activist should read Lee's essay. I discovered it when I was feeling absolutely battered by internal rifts in the women's movement. Reading and realising I was not alone was like discovering water in the desert. I contacted Lee, who kindly agreed to chat further over Skype from Seattle.

Part of the problem we're faced with, Lee suggests, stems from previous methods of feminist organising, notably the traditional idea of 'consciousness-raising' as central to campaigning.

'For the second wave of feminism, the idea of having a voice and taking up space was a very powerful tool. It was speaking back to power. It has continued into social media, with a sense that we individually assert our lived experience, that cannot be disagreed with.'

In other words, Lee believes that activists have adopted a sort of strategic essentialism as a political tactic: making other people listen by making them feel guilty or tugging on their heartstrings by speaking again and again about individual painful experiences. This has two drawbacks: it feeds an opposing narrative about 'snowflakes' who are hurt by everything (rather than fostering an understanding of structural inequality); and it ultimately dehumanises human experiences by making them simply fodder for arguments.

In fact, Lee argues: 'Feelings can't be centred. We have to make more space for reaction and discomfort and stay in the conversation. Your feelings don't matter! Our approach depends on debate skills rather than therapy skills.'

Dignity is important. We're all in the same conflict: we have all, to some extent, been traumatised by systems that hurt us. That makes it all the more important not to traumatise each other. Just because we know exactly which buttons to push doesn't mean we should push them. And remember more than anything that a hurtful, judgmental activist culture is not going to help us achieve our goals.

It can be very hard to put yourself out there only to see yourself taken apart and reassembled into pieces that no longer resemble the person you truly are. Who is big enough in that kind of battle to keep showing vulnerability and honesty? American performer and singer-songwriter Amanda Palmer sums it up in her song 'Bigger on the Inside': 'I am bigger on the inside/But you have to come inside to see me/Otherwise you're only hating/Other people's low-res copies.'

Rather than wasting time arguing who hurts the most and who is on the right side of history, let's make new spaces where we can, with respect and in privacy, test out our arguments and theories.

Deb Mashek is the executive director of Heterodox Academy, a non-partisan collaborative of professors and students across the United States that is committed to improving the quality and impact of research and education by promoting constructive disagreements among people with different points of view. She too warns that a movement that doesn't listen or make space for different opinions is going against its own core values.

'When we stop listening to each other, we lose what's most fundamental about our humanity, which is knowing and being known. When we're not listening, we lose that opportunity to know and be known, and as a community of learners we lose the insights and experiences and expertise and perspectives, which means we have to solve the problems absent some pieces of the puzzle.'

'There is a conflation in a lot of popular media and in a lot of the minds of the students that to feel uncomfortable is the same thing as to be unsafe. As a teacher, I know that learning doesn't happen unless you're uncomfortable, unless you've been unsettled. Learning happens in a space of discomfort.'

She reveals: 'We know from some of the surveys we've done that the students really fear if they say something wrong, or use a wrong word, it's going to show up on social media, it's going to be with them for the rest of their lives, somebody may have recorded it or set up a post about it. It feels very scary. You have to establish a basis of trust before you go into the hard conversations. Safe spaces to encounter ideas rather than to be safe from ideas, is the distinction one student made. Rather than being safe from ideas and perspectives, you can be safe to explore them in a way that's not going to follow you for the rest of your life if you get something wrong.'

Listening to Mashek talk about the conditions in which she teaches and in which her students feel comfortable to engage, I am struck again by how difficult we have made it, in so many circumstances, to be open and honest with each other; to be able to make mistakes and to learn and also to accept and take on board opinions that we might never agree with.

Mashek says her students end up making friends with people who see the world differently than they do. 'And I can't ask for much more than that.'

There are really very few spaces for activists to interact and feel safe in. It's particularly hard for women to express themselves freely, given that they are up against not just the policing of opinion we have looked at here, but are trying to do it against a constant background noise of misogyny and sexist trolling. When censure and disapproval is coming at you from both the inside and the outside, it's hard to know where to turn.

I feel like we need an internet for women. A place where we can discuss without trolls, or being watched, without fighting and judging and giving each other points for purity. So I sit down with Martha Lane Fox, the digital entrepreneur who first came to prominence when she founded online travel firm Lastminute.com during the internet boom of the late 1990s, and who most recently founded Doteveryone.org.uk, an independent think tank championing responsible tech for a fairer future. I ask what she thinks of this idea.

'Safe spaces where women can talk to each other are important,' Lane Fox says. 'Wikipedia is 85 per cent male editors; women's voices are quieter on social media; all the robots seem to be women – from Siri to Alexa – and when you look at the dynamics of the industry, all the money goes to male founders, partly because there aren't many female founders and partly because there is lots of sexism. A social network for women only might work, but I don't think that's the answer. It's got to be that women are co-designing all space and places so that different conversations are happening. When I look at

Twitter [where she sits on the board], the reason they didn't jump on the abuse quick enough was because they were a lot of white men, and they just didn't face it.'

'An internet for women might be great. But it would be much better if the internet was for everyone.'

So we have to get creative. We have to make our voices heard so that we can transform existing spaces and create new spaces where multiple perspectives can co-exist. As activists we have to be creators. And it can be really hard to find inspiration when we are working in such challenging environments, as Lee's experience illustrated. But that is precisely when we must remind ourselves how much we are needed. Toni Morrison's essay, 'No Place for Self-Pity, No Room for Fear', stemmed from her feeling that she couldn't go on with her work after the presidential re-election of George W. Bush. But before long she realised: 'This is precisely the time when artists go to work. There is no time for despair, no place for self-pity, no need for silence, no room for fear. We speak, we write, we do language. That is how civilizations heal. I know the world is bruised and bleeding, and though it is important not to ignore its pain, it is also critical to refuse to succumb to its malevolence. Like failure, chaos contains information that can lead to knowledge – even wisdom.'

Storytelling is a vital and optimistic form of advocacy for groups that experience discrimination. The media is one of the most powerful cultural tools we have as activists. But as we may seek to use it for positive change, the powerful media organisations that own these tools, and more, use them against us – dismissing and demeaning groups of people whose perspective has never occurred to or does not interest the overwhelmingly male news editors and moguls. Instead, they tell their own stories, that reflect and sustain their own power.

Speaking, writing and sharing our own stories, and insisting on many-sided reporting is key to opening up the world, challenging media bias and inaccuracy that shores up discrimination, exposing who holds power and taking the power of storytelling back for ourselves.

This is something that Liv Little understands very well.

'I was studying politics and sociology, and I was interested in women's issues. The university was very white, and everyone there was quite privileged, and people had very different views to myself. The curriculum that shaped the discussions was really monolithic and very Eurocentric and not something that I thought was rooted in the reality of what was happening. After two years of being in that environment, I was coming home in tears. I found it quite isolating ... I've always been quite a creative person, so I started to think, "What can I do from a personal level? I'm suffering. I'm not seeing myself represented."'

Little, a 25-year-old South Londoner, has achieved considerable success in creating a space for women and non-binary people of colour to see themselves represented. Her fledgling media empire gal-dem has grown from an online site to a magazine with a print run that has grown 50 per cent year on year and has editions in the UK, Holland, Sweden and Taiwan. Little has also recently been working in commissioning at the BBC's factual department.

At her lowest point, back at university, Little was inspired by British filmmaker Cecile Emeke, whose documentary

Strolling asked people of colour in Britain about their experience navigating multiple identities. Emeke had also created a YouTube series about two young black women. Little says, they were just 'living together and making jokes and being young – and there was no ulterior motive. I'd never seen young black female protagonists just being themselves.'

She started to put calls out for like-minded women with only a vague idea of what she wanted to create – 'some sort of online hub and eventually an online magazine and events and whatever. I found it surprisingly easy to find women who wanted to be part of it – even before there was anything concrete for people to like and see, we were managing to get a few thousand people liking what we were doing, and there was this excitement that finally space for women of colour was being carved out.'

Gal-dem received rave reviews. It provided a space for women and non-binary people of colour to talk about their lives – their experiences of race or cultural difference – and also to talk about politics, art and current affairs. As *Dazed* magazine put it when the first print magazine was launched: 'The magazine is refreshing, uplifting, hilarious and knows its audience intimately.' Or as Charlie Brinkhurst-Cuff, gal-dem's head of editorial, said back then, gal-dem was aiming to reach 'the type of teenager who is fed up with looking at skinny white women and vapid sex columns'.

Little says to me now: 'I think it's quite reductive when people say that feminism is simply about equality, because obviously within that there's so many intersecting identities and different struggles that emerge. Feminism is, for me, about recognising and celebrating the difference in the very, very vast category that is women – it's all about education.'

Perseverance means working at the same goal, but it also means working at the same goal in different ways and over time. One of the things that many of the activists in this book have in common is their capacity to come at a problem from many different directions, to experiment with approaches to see what works. Hard work makes its own luck. And being strategic gives you practice in all the different ways you can make that luck.

In her book *Grit*, Angela Duckworth reminds all of us activists that success results from effort combined with commitment. It sounds so obvious, but we so often forget this in a culture that celebrates 'natural talent'. We consider there's something special about people who are born good at doing something. But isn't there something equally – possibly more – impressive about people who become good at doing something from hours and days and weeks of relentless focus on it? (And, frankly, isn't that often what's behind the talent we so often thoughtlessly label as 'natural'?) Take heart from this. Don't be overwhelmed by thinking you don't have the necessary skills.

So much of effective activism is about allowing yourself to be open to new experiences and opportunities to learn. One of my friends worries that she hasn't found the thing she's good at yet. She often feels stressed and sad that she doesn't appear to have a 'talent'. Her search for meaning in the way in which she engages in the world has led her to travel, to do many different forms of work, to take up countless activities and hobbies.

Of all of my friends, she is the most immersed in the world. She is a seeker of boundless curiosity. Her heart is immense. And that, to me, seems a wonderful and meritorious talent in itself: to be constantly aware of the myriad opportunities and experiences around us.

You don't know what skills and talents you have until you start; furthermore, when you start to make an effort, you both discover your skills and make those skills productive. As Duckworth puts it: talent × effort = skill, but skill × effort = achievement.

Perseverance, like empathy, is something you can grow. Any good organisation that is developing new learning, building a new project or creating a product, builds in 'test and reflect' exercises. These have huge benefits in taking the sensitivity out of failure and accepting and embracing it as an experience that can bring positive understanding. By using this same practice as activists, we can develop the skills and processes that we need to learn and create. In short: disappointments and setbacks teach us new approaches and adaptations. They also teach us to prioritise.

'Grit grows as we figure out our life philosophy, learn to dust ourselves off after rejection and disappointment, and learn to tell the difference between low-level goals that should be abandoned quickly and higher-level goals that demand more tenacity,' says Duckworth.

Once you've committed to keep going, there are four ingredients for growing grit, Duckworth says: interest in your work, practising it regularly, doing it with purpose that stems from a conviction that it really matters, and hope, which, as we have already shown, is the secret ingredient for every successful activist.

I'd add a couple of other things. As a marathon runner, one of the most elemental things I learned about taking on a challenge is that sometimes it's simply about keeping going. Just putting one foot in front of the other. Yes, you need to practise to grow your muscles and stamina; you need to hope you can finish; you need to know that you're doing it for a good cause; and you need to develop your mental strength in order to bat away the voice that tells you to give up at Mile 23. But sometimes you simply need to just keep running.

And the best way to do that is to see yourself as part of a bigger picture. Contrary to appearances, individuals don't run marathons – teams do. Whether it's a group of charity runners all collecting money to hit the fundraising target, or elite runners backed by trainers, therapists and sponsors whose successes are all interlinked, it's teams that win the race.

So, when you're feeling tired or dispirited, try to remember that someone else is ploughing on and making great progress. While they're doing that, you can concentrate on the basics rather than setting the best pace. Similarly, when your energy is restored, it can lift someone who is feeling really tired and sore.

Being the leader of the Women's Equality Party was the most extraordinary experience of my life. But in order to grow the movement and also personally be able to keep going as an activist for women's equality, I had to eventually step away from that leadership position. I had to look for a different approach within a different collective, while working towards the same goal. I needed time to recover my strength. I needed time to be sad about the stories I had heard and the experiences I had seen and some of the feelings I had. I needed to nurse the embers of my activism that had cooled.

Doing the same thing over and over again and expecting a different result is the definition of madness. Doing the same thing over and over again without allowing yourself to take a break or try a different approach will risk tipping you into madness.

Finding practical support and encouragement in those with shared experiences is central to the success of the next activist model we'll look at.

Fiona Mavhinga grew up in rural Zimbabwe. Her family lived twenty kilometres away from her school and struggled to meet the cost of sending her to be educated. They sent their daughter to live with her grandmother, closer to the school, and the two of them would get up at 4am every morning to sell vegetables at the market in order to raise the money for school. After the market, Fiona would walk to school, do a day's worth of lessons, then return home to work on her grandmother's vegetable plot. Her mother also sold food to raise money towards the school fees. And her uncle and cousins would carry the little girl part of the way to school when she got too tired to walk.

'Growing up poor and in a marginalised community robbed me of my childhood,' she tells me. 'I had to work together with my mother and grandmother to be able to have school supplies and requirements. Most often, I was at the brink of dropping out of school.'

Fiona Mavhinga nonetheless finished school and went on to university with the help of a bursary from CAMFED, the Campaign for Female Education, which also put in her in touch with other young women who were going on to further education with the help of financial support. She explains that the combination of practical support and finding friends with similar experiences was what drove her to campaign in turn for other girls. She wanted to use the community investment she had experienced from her family to build further community investment around other girls. She is now a programme director at CAMFED and focused on paying forward the support that she received as a girl. '[CAMFED] enabled us to get together and out of that was born a sisterhood. The passion was to multiply the investment in our education for others living in the same circumstances that we had. And our strategy was to give ownership of the cause to local communities to ensure sustainability.'

Practising perseverance, according to Fiona Mavhinga, is about embedding your cause with local people who will support your work and enable you to carry on. It is also underpinned by setting values from which you won't depart. 'Our aim is to ensure each and every vulnerable child remains in school, and to activate all local support,' she says. 'Values inform strategies. Integrity, urgency, respect for local communities, child protection and accountability were ours from the beginning.'

When talking about the risk of activists feeling overwhelmed by the size of the job ahead, she says: 'Remember the cause, always. There are over 130 million children out of school across the globe. Any year we miss getting them into school and providing quality education is not only an economic loss but a refusal to give them human dignity and justice.'

The adversity that Fiona Mavhinga experienced as a child is very clearly linked to her activism: as she faces the job of helping other children, she is clear-eyed about both the difficulty and importance of her task.

Adversity – the scale of the job, or the pain of being challenged, or the pain of reliving the personal experiences that brought you here – can often provide clarity. Breakthroughs can be excruciating. But that intensely personal experience can also work to keep reminding you of the wider work that you are part of.

Ece Temelkuran, who we met on page 24, has been through it as an activist. She has repeatedly challenged Turkey's strong-man President Recep Tayyip Erdoğan and his administration as it grabbed executive power and sought to dismantle checks and balances by imprisoning lawyers, public workers, media professionals, military personnel, artists and many more dissenters framed as treasonous plotters. Temelkuran has been systematically threatened, harassed and discredited in her work as a journalist. When I ask her how she keeps going, she frowns:

'I do not think that I am keeping on going. I am wondering right now whether I should talk about that time in Tunisia when I lay on the ground because I was so exhausted from crying. Do I start with the pain or the part where I went through everything and then found myself in an emotional state of mocking my frustration?'

The misinformation and bullying levelled at Temelkuran by the political regime she challenged was so extreme as to be almost comical, she points out. 'In Australia, I was giving a speech about the concept of lying. I said: "I am a German spy. I am also a British spy. Also the Iranians hired me." And nobody laughed. I was so shocked that nobody laughed. And then I said: "For a while I was also a concubine for a Saudi sheikh," and then people started laughing. All of these were just some of the lies that were made up about me during the discrediting process organised against me.'

Though she may joke about that period, Temelkuran says she is still traumatised about it and is very aware of her ongoing emotional response to it as it manifests in her current behaviour: 'I notice now that whenever I feel some emotional comfort or a bit of security in terms of my job and how I live, I get so anxious that I realise I need – I am addicted to – that survival mode. Whenever I feel comfortable or secure, I have to think of the dangers that I might face, or horrible things that might happen to me, in order to feel comfortable under my skin.'

However, although she remains deeply affected, Temelkuran has managed the extraordinary act of under-standing her trauma as something impersonal, not rooted in an essential flaw of her own, but something deliberately used by her opponents to silence dissent. She perseveres by seeing her place in the bigger picture.

'The way to heal the bruises that these attacks leave on you is to look at them from a distance and to know that it's not personal. It's not about you. It's about the system. It's about history, it's about politics, it's about the position that you hold. And when I think like that, I can make my personal history a part of human history – which is so big a thing that I feel, in a very secure way, small.'

To hear Temelkuran speak of the lies her former colleagues made up to discredit her in order to save themselves, of the heartbreak she felt because of the crisis in her country, is to be frightened and inspired simultaneously.

I wonder what we can possibly do to resist and to halt the flow of such poisonous ideology, and she says simply: 'Action means old school political action. It means being on the street. Because the street teaches you the things you can't learn from books. It teaches you your limits and your limitlessness.'

So, when you're wondering what to do, or what to do next, or how to keep going, remember that sometimes simply to pro-test is an essential part of perseverance.

Temelkuran explains: 'Many people fear more when they are at home. Once you're on the street, you become fearless. One is surprised and shocked how one can be so fearless and limitless. That's why I propose understanding through action because without action the limits of understanding, and espe-cially understanding yourself, are so narrow, you do not know what you are capable of. But once you join political action out in the open, the hidden sources of your political soul and your capabilities as a political subject reveal themselves.'

'The only joy that activates human beings are other human beings. Being one with human beings. And that energises you, that makes you a courageous person. The simple joy of being together.'

The trust and love of other people is not something that can be achieved by following a set of rules about behaviour. I can't write a book for you about how to make people trust and love you. It's barely possible to comprehend the generosity of others when they bestow those gifts upon you, whether you're an activist or not. But what I have witnessed many times is that there is something essentially good in people, which is triggered when other good people stand up. And I believe that the challenge of being an activist is both to give and to find that trust and love in others.

When I look at my youngest daughter, who is in the first decade of her life, and has accompanied me on many protests and then come home to play with her dolls and her building bricks and her art set, when I consider the importance of her love and trust in herself and in others with whom she will build the next generation, activism feels like the only responsible choice as a human being, never mind as a parent. I feel it's important that I model these things for her, as part of trusting in other people's kindness and goodness, as an antidote to all the other voices telling us to be tough, to stop expecting much of human beings, to accept that life is hard.

Life can feel hard, but you don't build your strength for it by fighting. Nourishment comes from love and trust and finding it in each other. And that's where we find again our common good – at the heart of the relationships we make with one another.

Bana al-Abed is exactly ten days older than my Betty. She also likes to play the same simple games, but her time is divided between doing this and talking to politicians, educators and campaigners around the world. This has been her activism since she first captured the public's attention by sending desperate messages on social media from her besieged home-town of Aleppo. In September 2016, she and her mother began tweeting messages of fear and hope, interspersed with pictures of family life, and their hour-to-hour survival with little food and water, as they endured an unrelenting bombing campaign that included bunker-buster, phosphorus and cluster bombs.

In early October 2016, Bana tweeted: 'I am very afraid I will die tonight. This bombs will kill me now.' The following night she tweeted: 'Stop the bombing now, I want to sleep. I'm tired.' On another day: 'Dear world, can you see how big these bombs are?' and on another, an update from her mother Fatemah read simply: 'Hello world, we are still alive.'

As Western media seized on the story of the little girl who was shaming the world over its inaction on Syria, Bana and her mother were denounced as terrorists or tools of them by Syria's President Bashar al-Assad, as rebel propagandists by other critics and as 'fake news' by conspiracy theorists. Throughout bombing campaigns and disinformation campaigns alike, Bana and Fatemah steadfastly defended their story and the activism necessary to bring attention to what was happening in a part of the world closed to journalists, while global political leaders remained locked in paralysis over what to do about this multi-sided armed conflict, a proxy war of ancient grudges between multiple countries that, to date, has left more than half a mil-lion people dead or missing.

Bana and Fatemah al-Abed talk to me from Turkey, where they have been given permission to resettle after escaping Aleppo. Having made it to safety, Bana remains committed to sharing her experiences, and she tells me the story she has now told so many times, without hesitation.

'I was always seeing children dying. This is why I wanted to tell the world. I asked my Mum, "Is there any way to tell the world this story?" She said: "Yes, we can do something." So we started tweeting. We were under siege. I really felt scared. My school was destroyed. I went to many different schools, and then I couldn't go to school because they were all bombed and I couldn't go outside. My best friend died. I was so sad. At night there was always bombing and screaming, and I was always seeing fire. There were people running on the streets.'

As we're talking, the picture grows fuzzy and the screen freezes. But Bana's voice continues clearly: 'I am talking until the children live in peace. I want to go back to my country and build it up.'

Such perseverance at such a young age seems remarkable, but Bana doesn't see it this way. She says: 'My road is straight, and I am staying on it. Everyone can change the world. Everyone can do it.'

Fatemah al-Abed echoes her daughter's belief in continuing their advocacy. She says: 'We have to talk about what we faced, what no child should have seen. We can't build a future without our children. We have to focus on their lives and how we can make it different for them.'

'We keep faith in trust and in love.'

This right here is the essence of it all. Activism is trusting that the world can be a better place and loving the people who take this leap of faith with you. Trust and love underpin every rule of rebellion. And every rule of rebellion adds up to a philosophy of life that will sustain us no matter where in the world we are.

Activism is a state of mind. It's the intention you set at the start of every day. Difficulties, setbacks and outright failure do not alter that intention to rebel. The hardest thing you'll ever do as an activist is to commit to that. It will challenge you and test you. But it will also bring you fully into contact with the world – with the very best people, the biggest hopes and dreams, and the widest spectrum of human experience – and it will sustain you like no other decision.

The only thing left to do now is to commit. Declare yourself an activist. Join the rebellion of everyday, (extra)ordinary people who want to make something better.

Here's my hand.

Together, let's change the world.

NOW DO IT

If you want to make a change, make a list.

If you're feeling fired up and ready to go, ordering your thoughts can help you feel more in control. A list can give you a structure for the way in which you want to start being an activist. It can help you identify the problem you want to resolve and how you might set about resolving it. It can help you think about what you need for a good first campaign. And a list can help you see how far you're progressing. The lists below are just suggestions to help you make your own; the more detail you can think through at the start, the more likely you are to successfully plot your own rebellion.

A LIST FOR GETTING STARTED:

- What change do you want to see?
- What can you personally do about it? (If you were to break it down into initial steps what would the first three be?)
- How much time can you give to this project (hours a week)?*

- How long do you think this project needs? (weeks a year)?**

- Who do you know (friends, family, colleagues) who'd be really good at this and/or excited by it?

- Are any organisations already doing this work that you can team up with?

- What difference would this change make to your community and which community leaders might be willing to do this work with you?

- Do you need any more information about how to do this?

- Where can you find that information?

- Have fun!

A LIST OF POINTS TO REMEMBER:

- Organising a petition is not the same thing as running a campaign – it's useful first step to building awareness and putting pressure on decision-makers.

- Writing to your local and national political representative is also not a campaign, but it's a useful way to find out if you have an ally there and can be great for growing your network.

- Turning up in person always makes a difference. Emails and phone calls can be quick and efficient, but looking someone in the eye can build a bond that's stronger and longer lasting.

- Delegating helps other people to feel closely involved in the work and able to bring their own passion to the project. Don't hold it all too close. (And assign to yourselves and each other the tasks that you're good at – not just the ones that are the most fun! Deploying your skills in the best place makes for more efficient activism.)

- Look after your health. If things get stressful, step away for a bit, breathe and rest.

*Be honest with yourself!

** Don't be outfaced, nor push yourself too hard too fast. It's better to set yourself a realistic longer-term goal.

STAY INSPIRED

SOME LAST WORDS TO LIFT YOU

'To get started, follow your passion. I did that while waiting tables for a while. When I got out of college and I knew I didn't just want to get a job to work 40–60 hours a week about something I didn't care about, I was happy to work in the service sector while I volunteered with various activist groups to find what really drove me. Find a way to support that until it supports you.'

   – Ilyse Hogue, President, NARAL Pro-Choice America

'There was a degree of falling into it and figuring out what was needed that just kind of came. The most fundamental thing is finding the right people to go on that journey with you. No one achieves great things on their own.'

   – Liv Little, filmmaker, entrepreneur and founder of gal-dem media

'Look at it at a micro level. Think about your own family. When you have families with secrets, families who have unresolved issues – even if they try to paper over it and pretend everything is fine, it never really is until you address the core problem and the root of the issue. Once we fight through that discomfort and look at the problem honestly and head on, that's when we can begin to create long-lasting changes.'

– JUNE SARPONG, presenter, author and co-founder of the Women: Inspiration and Enterprise network

'Being 25 helps because you have a different sense of possibility and risk. So try to channel what you felt when you were 25! Also, do some things that make you feel uncomfortable, but say no to a lot of stuff and do things that make you feel happier. If you preserve yourself, then the things you really want to do will pop up.'

– MARTHA LANE FOX, digital entrepreneur and philanthropist

'Play Pandemic, not Monopoly. It forces you, instead of hoarding property and extracting rents, to collaborate to rid the world of disease.'

– KATE RAWORTH, economist and author of *Doughnut Economics*

'Imagine yourselves like the superheroes in DC comics. Bands of comrades working together. It has to be fun and celebratory – because it's also bloody hard!'

– PAM WARHURST, community leader and environment worker

'We complicate these things so much – but at the end of the day, organising is that feeling you had as a child and you realise that something on the news is really unfair and you ask your parents why. And the more of oppression you face, the more you are going to feel that sentiment from so many directions.'

– MINNA SALAMI, writer and organiser

'The first thing is finding your own community. If you look around, you'll find them. Your vibe attracts your tribe. People are around you that are vibrating on the same level of energy as you. Deep down we all know our life, what we're about, and a lot of the time we're too scared to say it. Once we really get to grips with what the truth is, the courage is just being that person.'

   – FEARNE COTTON, presenter and mental health campaigner

'I've given myself permission that I don't have to respond to everything that people say, to allow them to put me into a stressed-out reactive position. I think that that is a form of activism: refusing to be upset by people who either intentionally want to upset us or have a complete empathy gap or a lack of awareness of how these issues come across.'

   – PARIS LEES, campaigner for trans rights and journalist

'How to survive? Breathe and smile. What works? Compromise and conversation. Nobody's ultimately going to get whatever they want. We can't all get what we want. But if you compromise, you might get some of it. So look at the key points. Look at what's essential.'

   – NIMKO ALI, co-founder and CEO of The Five Foundation to end FGM

'We have not learned from history. Black and Asian people are still allowing themselves to be tribalised against each other. They're flattered, given positions of power, and so we remain as weak as we were. You could tell a similar story of women's rights and the rights of the poor. We will only overcome this when we have a truly inclusive rainbow class collective to face this juggernaut that's coming towards us; when we have a broad alliance of people who believe in fundamentals, for whom difference is not their defining feature.'

– Yasmin Alibhai-Brown, author, columnist and broadcaster

'At Greenham Common, I learned about the issues and the arguments from talking to the people who were there. There's a place for women's groups again so we can talk to each other. So often, women can't get to do this because they are carers or working in jobs that are inflexible. But the opportunity just to be together really matters.'

– Tulip Hambleton, women's equality campaigner

'I think we just don't talk about what challenges men. When I talk to different people across different organisations, I always start from: What's really going on? Don't tell me your stock answer. There are so many fears and concerns. Concerns about flexible working, babies, getting married – all those things that apply to women are concerns that men have. And yet we don't talk about them. Or we make them feel bad for even thinking about them.'

– Pamela Hutchinson, global head of Diversity and Inclusion at Bloomberg

'We care too much about women at the top. If I hear the term "glass ceiling", it is like chalk down a blackboard to me. Because there are women at the very bottom who we're not fighting for. I don't think that equality can ever work when there are women at the bottom who have been completely forgotten about. We have to talk about liberation.'

– Julie Bindel, writer and co-founder of Justice for Women, which helps women who have been prosecuted for killing violent partners

'I don't think people understand what the meaning of "diversity" is any more. It's a safe word to use when people are afraid of talking about really ugly things, like why most of the women in this world are not educated and don't know their rights. To progress we have to find ways of telling our stories. So long as your story matches somebody's idea of you, it keeps them absolutely safe and everyone goes away thinking: that's their world. The moment you start to make parallels, then you have somebody saying, "Oh my God this is not about a brown person far away; this is about somebody right in front of me."'

– RANI MOORTHY, playwright and actor

'Paula Gunn Allen, a Native feminist poet, warned the modern women's movement that "the root of oppression is the loss of memory". So, along with daily activism, we challenge history and its first draft in media and on the web. And we tell each other, learn from and discover we're not alone because we tell our own stories.'

– GLORIA STEINEM, feminist icon

'What keeps me going is remembering that this should be fun and we should find joy. We get disappointed by each other as activists, and we have to make relationships that go beyond the problem. That might look different for different people. As a queer trans person, for me that means making the whole room dance to Whitney Houston or having a lip sync battle.'

– NIM RALPH, activist, trainer and facilitator

FURTHER READING
FOR REBELS

To defeat despair:
Man's Search for Meaning, Viktor Frankl (London: Rider, 2004),
    New edition.
Learned Helplessness: A Theory for the Age of Personal Control,
    Christopher Peterson, Steven F. Maier & Martin E.P.
    Seligman (Oxford: Oxford University Press, 1995), New
    edition.
The Ethics of Ambiguity, Simone de Beauvoir (New York: Open
    Road Media, 2018), Kindle edition.
A Girl Called Jack, Jack Monroe (London: Michael Joseph, 2014)
Middlemarch, George Eliot (London: Penguin Classics, 2003),
    Revised edition.
How to Lose a Country, Ece Temelkuran (London: Fourth Estate,
    2019)
Slay in Your Lane, Yomi Adegoke and Elizabeth Uviebinené
    (London: Fourth Estate, 2019)
Happy, Fearne Cotton (London: Orion Spring, 2017), Reprint
    edition.

To channel rage:

Anger is Your Ally, Bina Breitner (Tuscon: Wheatmark, 2017)

What We're Told Not to Talk About (But We're Going to Anyway), Nimko Ali (London: Viking, 2019)

Letter from Birmingham Jail, Martin Luther King (London: Penguin Classics, 2018)

The Natural Way of Things, Charlotte Wood (London: W&N, 2019)

Rage Becomes Her, Soraya Chemaly (London: Atria Books, 2019), Reprint edition.

The Feminine Mystique, Betty Friedan (London: Penguin Classics, 2010)

Black Box, Shiori Itō (Beijing: CITIC Press, 2019; Arles: Philippe Picquier, 2019), Only available in Chinese and French editions.

Anger and Forgiveness, Martha Nussbaum (New York: OUP USA, 2019), Reprint edition.

To wield hope as power:

Hope in the Dark, Rebecca Solnit (Edinburgh: Canongate, 2016), Canons edition.

My Life on the Road, Gloria Steinem (London: Oneworld, 2016)

Selections from the Prison Notebooks, Antonio Gramsci (Independently published, 2018)

To collaborate with compassion:

Team Human, Douglas Rushkoff (New York: W.W. Norton & Company, 2019)

Why I'm No Longer Talking to White People About Race, Reni Eddo-Lodge (London: Bloomsbury Publishing, 2019)

Doughnut Economics, Kate Raworth (London: Random House Business, 2018)

Who Cooked Adam Smith's Dinner?, Katrine Marçal (London: Granta Books, 2016)

Sensuous Knowledge: A Black Feminist Approach for Everyone, Minna Salami (London: Zed Books, 2020)

Empathy, Roman Krznaric (London: Rider, 2015)

'Excommunicate Me from the Church of Social Justice', Frances S. Lee, 7 October 2017, https://www.catalystwedco.com/blog/2017/7/10/kin-aesthetics-excommunicate-me-from-the-church-of-social-justice

To practise perseverance:

Daring Greatly, Brené Brown (London: Penguin Life, 2015)

In Search of Silence, Poorna Bell (London: Simon & Schuster, 2019)

Grit, Angela Duckworth (London: Vermilion, 2017)

Dear World: A Syrian Girl's Story of War and Plea for Peace, Bana al-Abed (London: Simon & Shuster, 2018), Reprint edition.

ACKNOWLEDGEMENTS

A huge thank you to all the activists and campaigners who took the time to talk about their work for this book, and share their thoughts and tips. Thank you for the work you do and thank you for your encouragement to future activists.

Thank you to all the women and men who have offered advice and lent me courage and hope over the (continuing) course of my own activist learning. To the sisterhood within Reuters, the National Autistic Society, Women's Equality Party and Young Women's Trust who are working diligently every single day for change – thank you for your efforts and generous inspiration.

Thank you to everyone at the Blair Partnership who championed this book and helped me to get it out into the world – particularly my agent Jo Hayes, who first contacted me a couple of years ago to see what we might cook up together, then supported me through two jobs (me) and two babies (her) to finally write the book I really wanted to write. Jo: Thank you for all of your direction and encouragement. I can't wait to see what we do next.

Thank you to everyone at Icon Books, who loved this book as much as I do – the crack all-female team who have polished it, presented it and publicised it. Thanks in particular to Kiera Jamison, whose calm and thoughtful editing prompted some really educational conversations; and to Ruth Killick, who created so many great opportunities to have conversations with readers.

Thank you to my wonderful family. To my husband Chris: We celebrate ten years of marriage as this book comes out. It's been a quiet time, not much to test your patience, kindness, tolerance, good humour, inventiveness and mad parenting/cooking/DIY skills … I love you darling. To Grace and Betty: Precious girls, you are a constant source of energy, ideas and determination. I love marching with you, coming home to you and curling up with you. It's a privilege to be your mum. To my lovely stepsons Joseph and Daniel: Thank you for your loving encouragement and for being wonderful feminists. You give me hope for the next generation of young men. Thank you to my parents David and Lesley for always encouraging me to keep exploring; to my darling sisters Cathy and Harry for making me laugh til I can't breathe at just the point when everything starts to look too serious; and to my trio of delicious nieces – Esther, Ivy and Freda, the joy-bringers.

Thanks to the women we've quoted to inspire us and open each chapter, as well as throughout the book:

- Zadie Smith, *White Teeth* (London: Hamish Hamilton, 2000). Copyright © 2000 Zadie Smith.

- Lyz Lenz, 'All the Angry Women', *Not That Bad*, ed. Roxane Gay (London: Allen & Unwin, 2019). Copyright © 2018 Lyz Lenz.

- Rebecca Solnit, *Hope in the Dark* (Edinburgh: Canongate, 2016). Copyright © 2016 Rebecca Solnit.

- Ellen DeGeneres, source unknown.

- Maya Angelou, 'Still I Rise', *And Still I Rise* (London: Virago, 1986). Copyright © 1978 Maya Angelou.

- 'Bigger on the Inside', *There Will Be No Intermission*, Amanda Palmer (Amanda Palmer, 2019), https://amandapalmer.bandcamp.com/album/there-will-be-no-intermission. Copyright © 2015 Amanda Palmer.